GREEN INTERIOR DESIGN

The Guide to Sustainable High Style

SECOND EDITION

LORI DENNIS
& COURTNEY PORTER

ALLWORTH PRESS
NEW YORK

Allworth Press books may be purchased in bulk at special discounts for sales promotion, corporate gifts, fund-raising, or educational purposes. Special editions can also be created to specifications. For details, contact the Special Sales Department, Allworth Press, 307 West 36th Street, 11th Floor, New York, NY 10018 or info@skyhorsepublishing.com.

25 24 23 22 21   5 4 3 2 1

Published by Allworth Press, an imprint of Skyhorse Publishing, Inc. 307 West 36th Street, 11th Floor, New York, NY 10018. Allworth Press® is a registered trademark of Skyhorse Publishing, Inc.®, a Delaware corporation.

www.allworth.com

Cover design by Mary Ann Smith
Cover photograph by Stephen Busken
Interior photographs credited within captions
Interior illustrations by Vecteezy.com

Library of Congress Cataloging-in-Publication Data

Names: Dennis, Lori, author. | Porter, Courtney, author.
Title: Green interior design / Lori Dennis, Courtney Porter.
Description: Second edition. | New York, New York: Allworth Press, [2020]
    | Includes index.
Identifiers: LCCN 2020009717 (print) | LCCN 2020009718 (ebook) | ISBN
    9781621537632 (trade paperback) | ISBN 9781621537649 (epub)
Subjects: LCSH: Interior decoration—Environmental aspects.
Classification: LCC NK2113 .D48 2020 (print) | LCC NK2113 (ebook) | DDC
    747—dc23
LC record available at https://lccn.loc.gov/2020009717
LC ebook record available at https://lccn.loc.gov/2020009718

Print ISBN: 978-1-62153-763-2
eBook ISBN: 978-1-62153-764-9

Printed in China

CONTENTS

"It's not easy being green."

—Kermit the Frog

1
INTRODUCTION

There are plenty of reasons to "go green." But you probably already know that—that's why you're here! You want to know *how* to go green. When it comes to sustainability and green interior design, our firm has been walking the walk long before green was trendy.

Welcome to the second edition of *Green Interior Design*—the expanded sequel of the book we first published in 2010. The first edition featured lots of resources for design-build professionals, many of which were inaccessible to the general public. That's where this book is different.

Now, more than ever before, green has entered the mainstream. It's no longer just a fringe niche for new age hippies, it's a necessity for everyone. Homeowners of all backgrounds are savvier than ever, and if you're reading this, we know you're interested in making smart purchasing decisions for your home. We're here to help you do that—start to finish.

This book is infused with resources, green vendors to shop, and the best green interior design tips. Everything you'll find here is something you can implement. This book was a collaborative labor of love within our firm. We hope you'll enjoy it, interact with it, and share it with friends, family, and neighbors.

WHAT DOES GREEN MEAN TO YOU?

Perhaps up to this point, going green meant recycling water bottles, maybe even driving an electric car. With *Green Interior Design*, we want to challenge you to act bigger!

When you get into the weeds of building structures and furnishing your home, going green is not always going to be as simple as opting for paper straws over

plastic. So strap in and embrace the words of our friend Kermit the frog, "It's not easy being green."

A NOTE FROM LORI DENNIS

Green interior design is about living with intention and style. It's about having the realization that the decisions you make will affect the health and wellness of your planet, your family, and yourself. By reading this book, you've decided to make positive choices for your home, and to design a healthier and happier life.

Throughout most of my life, I've experienced the impact that interior design can have on a person and the environment. My ideas about green living were formed in the early 1970s. Like many American kids at that time, I was raised by very young parents who didn't have much money.

The kids I knew recycled bottles for spending money, ate everything on our plates at every meal, and had the leftovers for lunch the next day. Wasting was frowned upon. Lights were always turned off when you left a room. We wore hand-me-downs, and

our parents shopped at yard sales or thrift shops for household items.

When we did buy something new, it was a high-quality product, usually made in an American factory, by people who were paid fair salaries. These factories were governed by laws that protected the workers and the environment. This meant that the products were expensive and therefore needed to last. When these things broke, you repaired them.

I was also raised by a mother who honored the Cherokee part of our heritage. We viewed the Earth as a cherished thing to be treated with the utmost respect. Littering, being wasteful, or polluting has always felt inherently wrong to me. But I have always loved pretty objects and wanted to be surrounded by them—values our Cherokee ancestors held too.

My childhood bedroom was pretty bare. There were no decorations on the walls, and my bed was an ugly, green army cot, without a mattress on top of it. I didn't like being in that room; it was depressing.

But one day a set of Popeye cartoon sheets came in the mail, a gift from my aunt. The colorful sheets immediately transformed the room for me, turning it into a cheerful, bright place. I was actually proud of my bed after that. From that moment on, I understood how interior design could affect the way you feel about yourself and how you see the world.

Even as a kid, I noticed when things began to change in the 1980s. Western families became wealthy because of the expansion of credit. Factories rapidly began moving out of the West to third world countries where workers were paid unfair wages and there was little or no regard for their well-being or that of the environment.

Products became cheap enough to throw away and buy new. And as a result, the entire Western culture changed from being thrifty and mindful of waste to being okay with going into debt to buy disposable, cheap, toxic goods.

For the last four decades, manufacturers and consumers have been in a twisted relationship, where production and consumption matter much more than the pollution, illness, toxicity, and debt that's been created as a result. We've reached a point where the oceans are filled with plastic from household goods, electronics, and water bottles. Entire ecosystems are dying as a result of our overconsumption.

When you're sick and running out of resources, it makes sense to return to healthy approaches and conservation. And thankfully things have a way of going in cycles. Baby boomers are downsizing, unloading possessions instead of buying more. And because of the high cost of living and debt, an entire generation of millennials reside in smaller spaces, with fewer things.

Pop culture is also shifting. It's becoming cool to place less value on things and more value on experience and meaning in our lives. Popular TV shows like Marie Kondo's *Tidying Up* celebrate the joy of minimalism. Millions of people are opting out of purchasing or leasing their own private spaces to live and work, and instead chose to co-live and co-work in shared spaces.

Everyone has heard about being green, and millions of people are trying it out to see how it works for them. While we welcome you to jump in with both feet, be careful not to overdose. Our advice for getting started is don't try to learn everything on your first project. The amount of information is overwhelming to digest all at once. Thinking you can completely change to a sustainable way of being overnight is like joining a gym and expecting to have a six-pack the next day.

Remember that no project (or any built structure) is 100 percent green, not even the projects we share in this book. Try implementing some of the things you learn as you design or decorate your next project and improve on each subsequent one.

The most important thing to know is that training is critical. In addition to reading this book and the suggested additional reading, attend green building seminars, use experienced green contractors and trades, and graciously share your newfound knowledge with others as you learn and practice.

Get involved in your local community, and get involved in green decision-making when it comes to planning your city. Whew! Tired yet? That's all right. As you continue making your way through this book, you'll begin to feel confident as you learn more about the subject. You'll begin forming new eco-friendly behaviors. After time, they will become second nature.

Manufacturers, vendors, and the internet are making it easier, offering thousands upon thousands of green choices. We'd be lying if we told you all the products are as cheap as the mass-produced goods that usually come from China (with little or no regard to what effect the materials and manufacturing have on our planet and health). Still, as the demand for green products grows, prices continue to drop. So if you have to buy, buy green. We like to think of a time in the near future when we don't need to specify "green" anymore. Things will just be made with consideration for the environment and our health as common practice.

A NOTE FROM COURTNEY PORTER

You might be drawn to this book because your home looks something like the cover—or you may be part of the majority wondering, "If I don't have a big fancy house, is this book still for me?" The answer is a resounding "Yes!" Let's break through the three major blocks to green interior design and designing the aspirational home of your dreams: time, money, and trends.

Block #1: Time

Weekend mornings were spent making pancakes with my dad, while marathons of TLC's *Trading Spaces* played in the background. I was particularly fond of the episodes featuring ornately themed children's rooms. A Ruby's Diner–themed bedroom complete with a T-bird car bed and sparkly vinyl barstools? Ridiculous. Love it. I want in.

I wondered how in the world it was possible to create these magnificent spaces in a day with a $1,000 budget. *It's a lot easier when there's a full professional crew to install the space, and the resources of a production behind you*, my dad explained. The two biggest blocks to great design were already apparent: time and money.

Early on, I understood the truncating of time for the sake of TV drama. I understood they had to make time for the sponsors' ad breaks. I understood how much more efficiently things could be done by professionals but still wondered how long it would take me, a ten-year-old kid, to design and install a room like that.

I returned from a week away at fifth-grade science camp to find my dad redesigned my entire bedroom *Trading Spaces* style while I was gone. There wasn't a film crew to capture it, but I got my room reveal moment, and it was magical.

He stuck mostly to the show's rules as a test: he took the week to design and prepare, took a day to install, and kept any new additions under $1,000. That's what was possible for this non–design professional to completely transform the space (and this was before the convenience of online shopping swept the nation). The ceiling featured a hand-painted cloud mural—that part was hard on his back—and the center of the room was mostly taken up by my white metal-framed queen bed, an antique from my grandma's vast collection, which I still have today. Repurposing existing furniture and developing a love for long-lasting, quality antiques was my foray into sustainable design.

Block #2: Money

Throughout this book we'll cover projects of all scopes. Whether you're planning to DIY a studio apartment or hire a design-build firm like Lori Dennis, Inc. for your entire home—or something in between—the principles we discuss remain the same. But as you'll soon discover, even among projects of similar scope, each house has its own distinct personality hiding in its walls.

Through good design, we bring that out and make it a home. For these reasons, making sustainable design choices will vary with each and every project. Think of green on a spectrum rather than as a binary: Some things are more green than others. Some are as green as it gets! This book is a guide to get you thinking in this nuanced way. When you do, creativity starts flowing and work-arounds for the typical constraints of time and money will come as easily as the fun design decisions.

Block #3: Trends

There's another element of determining how sustainable a space is: how long you are going to like it before you're tired of it and want to tear it all out and replace everything. That's why designers, even outside the "niche" of green, are resistant to trends despite constantly writing about and commenting on them to stay relevant. Trends are fleeting. They are the opposite of sustainable. This should be lesson one.

This is also why terms like "timeless" and "contemporary" get thrown around in the design world. While those buzzwords *can* be the precise words needed to describe a home's style or a piece of furniture, oftentimes they are blanket statements conveniently bent to mean . . . whatever. Using these buzzy words proved particularly helpful when I dove headfirst into the deep end of the design industry seven years ago, without any formal education in design.

Rubbing shoulders with A-list designers at conventions and events around the country, I'd catch myself saying things like "Ooo that table leg—such a contemporary line!" while casually gesturing to a bunch of furniture on a showroom floor. I truly had zero idea what I was talking about, but I blended right in! (Now I am grateful for the past several years of on-the-job master class–level education in design and sustainability I didn't know I needed, from America's most inspiring interior designers!)

We'll use terms like these throughout the book. When you see language like this, personalize it. What is timeless for *you*? And seek not the easiest way to achieve it, but the most sustainable and thorough. You'll be well on your way to saving time, money, and the planet in the process!

WHAT IS "GREEN"?

"Green" is a term used to describe products or practices that have little or no harmful effects to the environment or human health. Most people have heard about recycling by this point but don't realize that the products they use have an effect on the environment from the point of extraction to manufacturing, shipping, packaging, use, and finally disposal.

Green companies seek to find products that are derived from renewable sources with minimal impact on the location of extraction. Care is taken in the manufacturing of the product not to add toxic ingredients that are harmful to human health or the environment in production, that is, chemical additives that will be dumped into a nearby waterway or landfill.

Consideration is given to using recycled materials in the product composition. The distance and method of shipping should be as benign as possible. When packaging a product, they choose environmentally friendly materials and use as little as possible to protect the product from the point of shipping to the consumer.

Green products can also be made with regard to the end of their useful life and companies may give instructions how, why, and where to recycle or dispose of them properly.

Another aspect of a green company is what they do with their success. How are the employees treated? How are profits divided? How does the community at large or the consumer who supports them benefit?

A traditional product or company focuses on providing a product that performs safely with the goal of making a profit. Green companies and products have the same agenda and take into account how they are impacting the earth and human health and well-being.

The goals of a green product or manufacturer are to preserve and protect the air, water, soil, wildlife, waterways, and food supplies by being conservative with natural resources and producing fewer toxins and less waste. They also strive to improve human conditions by giving back part of the profits they generate to communities and people in need.

INTERNAL CHECKLIST

The biggest sustainability challenge facing designers and homeowners today is understanding how the products they select truly impact energy use, the environment, and health. Understandably one of the first things people do when determining what to purchase is look at what products are made of and how easy they are to recycle. But rarely does one stop to think about the manufacturing process, transportation, or the installation of products.

So where do we start? And how do we measure how green something is or isn't? It's already complicated

enough to select beautiful, appropriate, and green items. To add another layer to the selection process—is it green enough?—makes the design process even more difficult.

Fortunately, as the green movement becomes more mainstream and more industries join the movement, it is getting easier. We are now seeing eco labels and ratings on products and projects.

These labels help us to determine characteristics of products:

- whether they contain recycled materials,
- whether the manufacturer uses resources and energy efficiently,
- how much pollution a product generates in its lifespan,
- any health concerns,
- water conservation, and
- whether it can contribute to LEED points and many more green qualifiers.

You may have seen the Energy Star Rated symbol on appliances you've specified lately or the WaterSense label on plumbing fixtures. LEED-rated buildings are also popping up all over the place—we're sure you've heard about or seen them. We've included a glossary at the end of this chapter to help you decipher what these labels and rating systems mean to you and your projects.

At our firm, we have two internal checklists we use when we begin a new project: the client/property checklist and the product checklist. As any good designer should, we thoroughly interview our clients about the obvious (what does the client want and need) and then go into the not-so-obvious areas of their personal health and green aspects of their project.

Remodeling or new construction can be driven by many factors. Our client may need more usable space. The space the client is in may contain outdated or worn furnishings and materials. Health concerns like allergies or asthma might play a role in the decision to make changes.

Internal Client Checklist

Human Health	☐ Are you experiencing coughing, sneezing, chronic fatigue, asthma, frequent headaches, dizziness, or any other unexplained symptoms?
	☐ Are these symptoms exacerbated by prolonged periods indoors?
	☐ Do these symptoms disappear when you leave for extended periods and return when you come home?
	☐ Are you aware of any mold? Humidity? Musty odors or mildew? Do houseplants have mold?
Reasons	☐ Why have you decided to go green? For environmental or health reasons?
	☐ How long do you plan to live in the newly designed space?
Size	☐ How much space does the client need? Is it really necessary?
	☐ What is occurring in these spaces?
	☐ Does the space plan take advantage of all usable space?
Natural Environment	☐ How can we take advantage of natural light and airflow in most, if not all, of the residence?
Materials	☐ What are your aesthetic preferences?
	☐ Do you have health/chemical sensitivities to certain materials?
	☐ Is there an opportunity to use salvaged materials?
	☐ Do you have materials or furnishings that you wish to reuse?
	☐ What is your attitude about cleaning and maintaining the property?
Insulation	☐ How can you seal the walls, ceilings, doors, and windows to prevent unwanted heat/cooling loss and gain?
	☐ Is noise pollution a factor?
Energy Usage	☐ Are the home's systems efficient? This includes lighting, appliances, water heater, heating/cooling.
	☐ Are current energy bills unusually high?
Renewable Energy	☐ Is there an option to install renewable energy systems? On what scale?
Water Conservation	☐ How can we minimize indoor water use and waste?
	☐ Are there options for rainwater collection?
Landscape	☐ What types of plantings are indigenous to the region?
	☐ How can you minimize or eliminate nonporous hardscape?
	☐ Is there an option for a green roof? Can it be used?
	☐ How does the client feel about an edible or cutting garden?
	☐ Can landscaping provide shade to the south and west sides of the home?
	☐ What are the opportunities for outdoor living spaces?

The following client/property checklist of questions helps us to determine how best to design in an environmentally friendly, health-based way that addresses the client's needs and allows them to live well in their new space. Adapt it for yourself!

Once we have established a good understanding of the issues driving the project and we are ready to begin purchasing, we refer to our product checklist.

The product checklist helps us to make the most sustainable choices by measuring eco products against conventional products and against other eco products as well.

Very few, if any, products will have a favorable answer to each of these questions. But the more yes answers you have on your list, the more confident you will be that you are selecting truly green products.

Product Checklist

☐ Is it locally produced?

☐ Is it grown organically?

☐ Does it come from renewable sources?

☐ Are there extraction methods with little or no impact on the environment or wildlife?

☐ Is it made of recycled or reclaimed materials?

☐ Has it been produced without toxic chemicals or ingredients so it doesn't off-gas or release toxins into the environment?

☐ During manufacturing were recycling methods used to eliminate waste?

☐ Does the manufacturing plant utilize energy-saving systems?

☐ Is it packaged minimally?

☐ Is it good-quality design that will last for a lifetime?

☐ Is it the most energy-efficient type of product of its kind?

☐ Is it adaptable? Can its life be extended to meet changing needs and tastes through upgrading or refurbishing?

☐ Can it be recycled at the end of its life?

☐ Does the manufacturer accept responsibility for taking back the product for refurbishing or recycling at the end of its useful life?

☐ Does it have a third-party green label?

VENICE ART HOUSE

Photos by Mark Tanner

HOME TOUR: VENICE ART HOUSE

You can't beat the location of Venice Beach and having an absolute dream client: an artist herself, Jodi Pantuck, boasts an expansive modern art collection. This project would be all about integrating both her personal art and the art she's collected and making that the centerpiece of the home. This home also encapsulates so many of the design styles we're best known for: it's modern, coastal, and made for the California indoor-outdoor lifestyle.

When you're a collector of any sort, it can be a tricky balancing act trying to go green. One of the biggest mistakes American homeowners make is in overbuying and hoarding. That doesn't mean you have to be a strict minimalist; this home certainly isn't. Even though it is modern and clean, in a lot of ways it's the exact opposite of minimalistic, with colorful art covering nearly every square inch of wall space. But everything serves a purpose and enhances the home and the moods of its inhabitants.

The stairs are one of those "wow" architectural features in the home that makes a statement when you first walk in, complemented by a Ralph Greco sculpture on the landing.

A bright white-and-color-infused living room makes this casual space perfect for entertaining. The wall space above the orange side table in the corner features two abstract works by artist Scott Yeskel—that of a pool and metal RV. His work is serving us some major Palm Springs vibes! Upon entering the home, you're also greeted with a row of paintings by Steven Keene above a row of Noir furniture cabinets that add a natural texture and modern, playful dimension to the space.

WHAT MAKES THIS HOME GREEN?

Sunny California to the rescue! Solar panels were installed on the roof. The home was constructed to allow maximum natural airflow and natural light-reducing electrical and HVAC loads. All the walls are insulated for warm air that comes in through the windows in winter to remain in the home with low-e glass windows.

All lighting is LED and on dimmers, and all the appliances are Energy Star certified. But the green element defining this home is its indoor-outdoor flow: large, dark-framed windows, popping against the home's sleek, white exterior. They remain open most of the time, allowing all the natural daylight to flood in and the sea breeze to blow through.

The edible garden in the front of the home was designed by talented local garden designer Christy Wilhelmi. She included flowering, indigenous plants to promote bee and butterfly propagation. The pavers make the garden easy to navigate and maintain. Plus she's growing her own food! Doesn't get much more sustainable than that. The home also includes gray-water garden systems for minimal environmental impact.

Cozy low-slung lounge seating from Teak Warehouse, made of FSC-certified wood with steel bases, not only makes this the perfect spot for entertaining, it's as weatherproof as you're going to get! It may be Sunny SoCal, but homes near the beach still take a beating from the moisture and salt in the air. These are sustainable pieces that stand the test of time.

Part of designing a good indoor-outdoor flow is carving out areas to create more intimate moments. A beautiful outdoor rug is a great way to segment off a space and add an enticing, visual element. Here it helped create a focal point among the many vibrant colors and the gallery wall. A great architectural feature using natural materials, like a wood-paneled wall, lends a

modern aesthetic and continues the indoor-outdoor theme vertically.

The painting on the art wall in the dining room of Satan the Cat is by Vanessa Stockard, whose work is moody and visceral, adding a deeper texture and comical element to the space.

Both the pomegranate art featured in the modern art house kitchen and the bee painting in the powder room are by artist Gus Harper, whose philosophy involves searching for the beauty in everyday objects.

Efficient toilets and faucets were installed throughout the home to reduce water usage. And water storage tanks for rainwater collection were installed.

Knowing your focal point is imperative in the design of any space, indoors or out. On the roof deck of this beautiful Venice Beach home, the focal point was obvious: the gorgeous panoramic view. So we did everything to not distract from that with low-slung, loungy outdoor furniture in muted, neutral color palettes. Designing an indoor-outdoor space is all about letting nature guide you.

Take a less-is-more approach. Think twice before purchasing accessories and furniture; your space will look cleaner and sleeker, and the environment will thank you too. Our rule of thumb is to choose five pieces of furniture you really love and need in a room and donate the rest. Editing is key!

"Conservation
is a state of harmony
between men and land."

—Aldo Leopold

2
FURNITURE AND ACCESSORIES

Most conventional furniture and accessories on the market today are made overseas with little regard for the raw materials that are wastefully excavated; the pollution that is created during manufacturing, packaging, and transport; or the unfair wages and working conditions many factory employees endure. A home is thought to be a haven, but if it is flooded with toxic materials, it's not exactly the idyllic retreat we imagine.

Typically, the wood, plastic, and fabric in most furniture is made or finished with toxic materials, so the furnishings selected to make a space livable actually create indoor air pollution that is harmful to human life. Toxic chemicals and organic pollutants used in paints, paint strippers, and wood preservatives routinely applied to household furnishings are suspected to cause cancer in humans and animals.

Formaldehyde, a known indoor pollutant, is used as an adhesive in most residential wood furniture. Polyurethane, a toxin known to cause cancer in humans, is used as a sealant in most residential wood furniture. Brominated flame retardants (PBDEs), linked to brain disorders and birth defects, are used extensively in household furniture, even though they have been banned throughout Europe.

All of these factors contribute to Sick Building Syndrome, which can cause dry or burning sensations in the eyes, nose, and throat; headaches; dizziness; fatigue; nausea; and memory loss. By selecting furniture and accessories from companies that use renewable or sustainably grown, nontoxic materials, follow environmentally friendly manufacturing processes, and engage in fair trade practices, you help diminish environmental and health hazards, and you continue to make green products more available and affordable.

REUSE WHAT YOU HAVE

Before you run out and buy anything new, consider using what you already have. Look closely at what can be cleaned, refinished, painted, repurposed, or reupholstered. A client of ours recently moved into a new home with a significantly different interior style. By making alterations to her existing pieces, she was able to reuse 95 percent of her furniture. The other 5 percent was sold at a yard sale and on Craigslist and donated to a women's shelter.

The client paid about one-tenth of what she would have to buy new things, and her house looks incredible. She was happy, we were happy, the planet was happy.

BUY THE BEST

If you were looking for permission to splurge—here it is! When selecting new furniture pieces, make sure to buy the best, most durable furniture you can given your budget. When it comes to furnishing a home, buying things that are made to last, things that don't have to be replaced, is one of the greenest game plans you can have.

When a piece of furniture can be passed down through generations, it prevents the need for raw materials to take its place, as well as manufacturing and disposal. (If this is the excuse you need to splurge, we're here to give it to you!) The advertising team at Sutherland Furniture says it best: "We hold the philosophy that the only thing better than recycling is

Bedroom by Lori Dennis. Photo by Ken Hayden.

could occur at the table over decades, however, the expense seemed more reasonable. After all, tables of this quality, in this condition, made by midcentury masters don't come along every day. Well kept, this table can become an investment that will likely appreciate in value.

to make something that never needs to be recycled." Today's purchases should be tomorrow's antiques.

When you have a stunning, sustainable piece that will last for many generations, you don't need to buy a new one. This Hollywood Hills bedroom is understated and grand all at once. Reclaimed railway ties add a lot of character to the bed.

Photo by Christian Romero.

Photo by Christian Romero.

Our client fell in love with these vintage abalone-inlaid R. J. Gibbings dining chairs and table. He wasn't, however, in love with the $17,000 price tag. When we discussed the amount of joyful dining that

Of course not everyone can afford a $17,000 dining table. These vintage rosewood table and chairs were purchased on eBay for about $1,500. It's just perfect for the client and can grow with his family, as it has a leaf and a total of six chairs.

SELECT GREEN MATERIALS

Choose furniture that is made with sustainable materials and little or no toxic finishes. There are many components to consider when making green choices for upholstered pieces; from the wood frames, glues, webbing, springs, foams, and cushions to the fabrics, each piece needs to be examined for sustainability and potential health hazards. Any wood element should be FSC certified from well-managed forests, and fabrics should be sourced from eco-friendly products.

Read labels before you purchase, and ask a lot of questions. Ask questions to the point of being annoying. Some vendors think they are making a green piece of furniture when in reality 85 percent of the piece could be toxic and imported from a place where workers are subjected to questionable labor environments.

NONTOXIC INGREDIENTS

A healthy living space is one that contains furnishings with nontoxic finishes. Instead of solvent-based finishes, which off-gas for years, choose water-based, no-VOC finishes. Foams are typically made with petroleum-based products, which have been linked to hormone disruption. This is frightening when you think of all the time you spend with your skin touching and absorbing these materials. The glues and frames of upholstered pieces often contain noxious chemicals, including formaldehyde.

FAIR TRADE

Unless we are buying from a local manufacturer, we don't usually think about the people who make our furniture. Many times these people are subjected to unhealthy work environments and risk their lives for a few dollars each day. It is imperative to buy from companies that practice fair and safe manufacturing processes.

Because so many, unfortunately, do not, green companies will make it clear when they are practicing eco-friendly economic and social behavior—just read their environmental statements. Often you will be able to identify "the good guys" with a fair-trade label. As an added bonus, companies that support local artisans and indigenous peoples tend to have unique furniture and accessories, which greatly enhance room interiors.

EASY TO CLEAN

Select furniture that is easy to keep clean. Well-maintained items will last longer and reduce the need for replacement. Dirt- and dust-free environments are also better for indoor air quality. Smooth, hard surfaces will be easier to clean than heavily detailed pieces.

If you are in a humid climate, avoid furniture that will absorb moisture. Slipcovers and fabric window treatments should be made of washable fabric or materials. Buy furniture and accessories that do not require routine application of toxic products.

ERGONOMICALLY CORRECT

No matter how perfect it looks, resist the urge to purchase furniture that is not comfortable or ergonomically correct. Sitting and sleeping pieces need to look good and provide excellent support. This is especially important in your work chair, where you might sit for long periods each day.

RECYCLE

We have never completed a project without searching at least one of the following: Craigslist, thrift shops, garage sales, consignment shops, antique stores, or eBay. Selecting salvaged, used, vintage, or antique pieces adds a charming quality to any interior. Depending on your budget, buying a used piece can be the most affordable or expensive purchase of your project. Either way, it will be the greenest.

Make this a habit on every project. Collectively we will eliminate millions of pounds of furnishings from entering the waste stream. On the flip side, donate unwanted furnishings, or give them away. Avoid throwing them away whenever possible.

The gorgeous wood table in this wine cellar was a $150 purchase from Craigslist. It's exactly what we were looking for, already painted, and could handle the red wine stains! (Photo by Erika Bierman.)

Incorporating antiques into any interior adds an immediate feeling of history, especially in a newly built space. M. S. Rau has gorgeous furniture, rivaling any European shop. If you ever get to New Orleans, make sure to visit them, as the smell and touch of these fine works of art are impossible to capture in a catalog or website. (Photo Courtesy of M.S. Rau, New Orleans.)

New life was sprayed onto this '40s vintage desk. The powder coat orange paint is virtually indestructible and brightens up the space! Office by Lori Dennis. (Photo by Ken Hayden.)

UPHOLSTERED PIECES

Our Favorite Places to Shop Sustainably Upholstered Furniture

Crate and Barrel (www.crateandbarrel.com) believes the best place to conserve and protect our natural resources is at home. Their American-made lines feature sustainable woods and renewable materials. They offer full-scale and smaller, apartment-sized furniture. The company is currently working on more eco-friendly initiatives in their product lines.

Crate and Barrel's affordable younger sibling CB2 (www.cb2.com) sells a smaller-scale, urban upholstery line with eco-friendly construction and materials. Some features include certified-sustainable hardwood frames, soy-based cushions, removable seat covers for cleaning, and organic fabrics. Their products are made in the United States.

Cisco Brothers (www.ciscobrothers.com) is an American manufacturer that has practiced social responsibility since the early 1990s by renovating abandoned warehouses and providing apprentice/employment programs in inner cities. Their hand-made furniture ranges in style from contemporary to

Tête d'Homme Barbu V by Pablo Picasso, via M. S. Rau.

traditional, and every piece is built to last. They use responsibly grown wood frames, reclaimed-wood legs, nontoxic fasteners and finishes, petroleum-free latex cushions, and organic or renewable fabrics colored with vegetable-based, low-impact dyes and laundered in chemical-free, vegetable-based detergents. The furniture is comfortable and attractive and can be made custom.

Elegant and modern, the Enzo banquette from Cisco is customizable to fit the right dining table. Pictured here in performance fabric that is easy to keep clean. All of their furniture can be made with an Inside Green option (organic) and treated to be stain resistant with an eco-friendly product. (Photo by Dunja Dumanski.)

Cisco brothers has been "doing sustainable" for well over a decade. They manufacture in refurbished warehouses, injecting desperately needed employment opportunities into depressed communities. When you look at the superior style of their transitional designs, you can't help but want a piece in your own home. They feel as good as they look, and they last and last.

Edward Ferrell + Lewis Mittman's Pure Collection (ferrellmittman.com) contains some of the most luxurious, well-made, transitional-style furniture available today. The company's long-term sustainable initiatives include manufacturing goods in North Carolina, employing an American workforce, and eliminating millions of tons of greenhouse gases required for overseas transport.

In their factory they have instituted a recycling and reuse program for excess materials and a water recycling system. The following sustainable materials are used in manufacturing: organic fabrics; soy-based cushions; low-VOC paints, adhesives, and finishes; FSC woods and veneers; renewable fibers like jute twine; and recycled-content nail heads.

Simply divine, stylish, well made and affordably priced, Mitchell Gold + Bob Williams (www.mgbwhome.com) is a vendor with a green heart. They support a long list of charities. The education-based center is a model for all American businesses with its superior equipment, learning, and nutrition plans. The company has been making eco-friendly furniture way before it was in vogue. Furniture is made from recycled-content and nontoxic materials, including recycled and recyclable packaging.

Furnature (www.furnature.com) has been making organic furniture since the early '90s. Their pieces are free of toxins, healthy for humans, and easy on the environment. Making affordable furniture that will last for many generations is one of their solutions to stop the poisoning of the Earth. They understand that environmental consciousness is no longer a choice but a necessity if we expect health and prosperity for future generations. This is also one of the few green manufacturers that offer traditional styles of upholstered pieces.

Ligne Roset (www.ligne-roset.com/us) is a French modern upholstery company that has been practicing sustainability since the '70s. They begin with a clean, low-toxicity manufacturing environment and produce products that don't create pollution in consumers' homes. The furniture contains no harmful solvents in finishings, no fungicides or biocides, no heavy metals, no formaldehyde, and no PBDEs or PBBs. Every piece is designed with thought given to how it can be recycled at the end of its life. The employees are French, so you can imagine how good they have it: cost-free at-work nurseries, ergonomic workstations,

HOME TOUR
BEL AIR ROAD

Photos by Mark Tanner

machines that eliminate noise pollution, and a lot of paid vacation days!

One of our favorite retailers, IKEA (www.ikea .com), has a never-ending list of socially and environmentally responsible acts. They make the top of the Sustainable Furnishing Council and National Wildlife Federation's Wood Furniture Scorecard, yet again!

From recycling centers in stores, to nontoxic products, to flat-pack shipping (which saves millions of tons of transportation-related greenhouse gases), to use of sustainable, recyclable, and renewable sources, to recycling food waste from its restaurants into energy sources, to powering plants with renewable energy sources, to donating products and money to charities throughout the world, to employing local artisans, to encouraging consumer conservation by not providing free plastic bags—seriously, we could go on and on!

They have excellent style and value for exceptional prices. And we'll let you in on a little secret: we use some IKEA products in nearly every project we design, even in a $12 million residence in Bel Air.

WHAT MAKES THIS HOME GREEN?

This house was in great shape, but the style was very dated. It was ornate, very '80s. Initially, the client wanted a completely modernized home and wanted to rip everything out. We were able to convince them that with fresh paint, new lighting, and their existing modern furniture, we could transform the majority of the home into one that worked for them without altering the existing structural and decorative elements like the reclaimed-wood ceiling beams, stone flooring, fireplace, and cabinetry.

In the bath and kitchens, we replaced inefficient plumbing fixtures with high-efficiency appliances. We kept the cabinets but replaced the counters with Caesarstone and replaced the existing plumbing fixtures. Good as new!

Even though there were two master closets and a considerable hall with shelving outside of the master bedroom, we needed a lot more room for our client's collection of over one thousand pairs of designer shoes. We decided to go into the hall and make it a kind of art installation, expanding her closet with glass shelving, which was really cool because it displayed the most beautiful shoes.

The $30,000 price tag from the cabinet builder was not a solution that the client was really happy about. So IKEA to the rescue! We installed floor-to-ceiling glass-faced cabinets all down the bedroom hallway for around $2,000. We love IKEA.

They have really good solutions with some of their closet and cabinet systems. They're affordable and durable. There's nothing that makes us happier than

To update the spaces, we replaced counters with easy-to-maintain-and-clean materials (Caesarstone) and matched existing marble in the tub that was replaced in the master for a more efficient soaking tub.

going high and low in the same project and putting something from IKEA in a $12 million Bel Air house. And in this case, their product completely solved the price and storage problem for us.

DESIGNING YOUR CUSTOM DREAM CLOSET: AN EXPLAINER FROM A NONFASHIONISTA

Close your eyes and visualize your dream closet: What stands out to you? Is it a colorful designer wardrobe? A vast purse and shoe collection? How organized everything is? How glamorously spacious it is inside?

Whether you're DIYing or hiring a design team for a custom renovation, before you begin designing your dream closet, you need to start by getting clear on what is going to go in the closet once it's completed. Admittedly, we are not clothes hounds, but we can appreciate a great wardrobe as much as the next.

I do design a lot of custom closets for our clients, many of whom have incredible wardrobes in need of storage. If you're like our iconic Bel Air fashionista client, before you even begin designing your custom closet, we implore you to go through a tough-love purge strategy and eliminate any clutter:

Part I: Simplifying Your Wardrobe

There should be a place for everything! Here are some of our personal favorite minimalism tips for purging your closet and simplifying your wardrobe.

Donate or Trash

Plan a clean-out day and be incredibly editorial—if you haven't worn/used an article of clothing in a year, throw it out, or, better yet, donate it to someone who will give it a new home! If you're throwing out a worn-out item, keep an inventory of what needs replacing. There are also places you can donate fabrics—not just clothing. In many cities, H&M will take any donated textiles and make sure they're donated

to the right places to be repurposed. How's that for fast fashion trying to course correct?

Sorting & Getting Organized

Once you have your "keep pile" finalized, pick a method of organization: sort by type of clothing and color or by occasion and season, whatever best suits your lifestyle—but choose just one so you're best able to keep track of everything you have. Then, pull out the items you use most frequently—you might want to give those their own "zone" in your new closet. Consider beginning your custom closet design by keeping these pieces stored at eye level and determining what is to be hung versus folded.

Purge or Discard Bag

This is perhaps the most important element because it's all about the sustainable part of the design. For ongoing maintenance, you might want to consider keeping a "purge" or "discard" bag or hamper in your closet to discard any other items you want to get rid of later, instead of continuing to store them. Another efficient way to weed out clothing items you don't wear is the old hanger trick: make sure all of your hangers are facing forward and when you find an article of clothing you don't wear often, face the hanger backward. Once you get in the habit of this, it'll be easy to maintain the organization of your gorgeous new closet!

Buying New Clothing

Next, with any new additions to your wardrobe, consider adopting a conscious consumer strategy that ensures you're also living green and sustainably when you are clothing shopping. The first major boom of online retailership gave us more access to fast fashion, an irresponsible way of manufacturing and selling clothing to mass markets at discounted prices, that comes at a pretty high cost to the environment and to the workers who make the clothing.

"Buy less.
Choose well.
Make it last."

—Vivienne Westwood

Of course, these fast-fashion retailers always existed, and the other thing the internet has been good about is influencing a backlash against fast fashion, with ample, affordable, transparent, sustainable clothing retailers like Everlane (www.everlane.com) and The Reformation (www.thereformation.com), to name a couple. Many contemporary fashion lines have clearly marked sustainability initiatives on their websites or on their clothing's tags.

When it comes to designing a closet, the most important thing to know before you begin is exactly what is going to go back into the closet when it's finished. All set?

Okay, let's move on:

Part II: Design Tips for Customizing Your Dream Closet

Some good news—you can actually shop big-box stores with off-the-rack shelving units relatively cheaply and sustainably! Just be sure to read online product reviews diligently.

Watch out for buzzwords like "wobbly" or anything about the edges chipping. But otherwise, you don't have to be too precious with the building materials used in your closet. Compared to kitchens and baths, where materials are exposed to wetness and extreme heats, messiness and high foot traffic, the closet is relatively low maintenance.

Closet Accessories

Designer accessories and add-ons are what give a dream closet that sought-after "wow" factor, but they are not cheap. Some of our firm's favorite things to include that really take the design to the next level are:

- sunglass dividers
- glass-top islands with see-through jewelry drawers and watch winders
- drawer boxes for undies, bras, jewelry, belts
- drawer and shelf dividers for sweaters, jeans, T-shirts
- shoe walls
- purse displays
- pull-out poles
- safes
- pull-out shelves/drawers
- mirrors

Adding Some Glam in Your Custom Closet

Some extra aesthetic touches that have nothing to do with storing or accessing your clothing will ultimately be what elevates your closet to dream status! This is where you get to have fun and customize! But you don't have to go crazy. You probably don't need all or even *most* of these bells and whistles. In combination, they're likely to get in the way. After all, a functional closet should be a one-movement operation. Here are a couple brilliant ways to do this:

Lighting

Light beyond your general task lighting: We love adding some sparkle with a twinkling chandelier and a full-length mirror, which is both functional and necessary in the closet/dressing area anyway. It has the added bonus of bouncing light around the space to give it that designer twinkle.

Wallpaper

Wallpaper is very in right now, and it's such a great way to get creative in your closet and make it your own. Especially if you're planning to buy cheaper for your storage and shelving units, consider splurging on the wallpaper to elevate the design. A great way to transform ordinary shelving and storage is by wallpapering behind it. And don't forget the ceiling! That's a great place to add a bold pattern or color. Sky's the limit!

We installed four $350 units from IKEA in this closet and jazzed it up with accessories and designer details like a bright lacquer paint and a boldly printed wallpaper.

Photo by Erika Bierman.

Rugs

Add a rug! No matter the size of your closet, having something soft underfoot adds richness and extra luxury to the space.

Part III: Storage Solutions for Organizing Your Dream Closet

Matching Space-Saving Hangers

A great rule of thumb is to keep your hangers spaced out a finger width apart, which makes finding clothing so much simpler.

This dressing room features the Lake Agawam wall covering from Calico, one of our favorite feminine prints.

Out-of-Season Clothing Storage

You'll want to keep all your no-wrinkle, knit items folded rather than on hangers to prevent hanger bumps in nonglass, closed, stackable containers, clearly labeled. Pro tip: Fold your clothes vertically rather than stacking them on top of each other for easier visibility and access. Too often, we forget about the clothes that end up folded on the bottom of a drawer.

Luggage and Purse Storage

Rather than hanging bags, keep them on a shelf, in dust bags and stuffed with tissue so they maintain their shape over time. Prominently displaying her designer bags and shoes was an important part of this recently completed project in Bel Air.

Shoe Storage

Shoe storage is an often-overlooked aspect of closet design, but shoes can potentially take up so much room if you have lots of them or can clutter up your space if you neglect to think about storing them ahead of time. Opt for shoeboxes with windows for more formal, expensive shoes, much like dust bags for purses and luggage and staggered shelving for easy access to shoes you wear most often. Casual walking shoes can fit two pairs to a box, or on staggered shoe shelving for easier access.

Jewelry and Watch Storage

Jewelry boxes with glass tops are going to be best for seeing what you're working with and keeping everything safe, and it makes getting ready more efficient.

Keep a catchall or two on your counter for rings, keys, and so forth. Avoid using drawers as catchalls so you prevent recluttering your closet after you've made it beautiful. This may sound anal-retentive, but it'll quickly become second nature, and you'll thank us later!

CASE GOODS AND TABLES

Sarreid Ltd. (www.sarreid.com) sells gorgeous wooden case goods, many of which are made from reclaimed pine—like this modern console. Their products can be purchased through Sarreid Gallery Dealers.

Using FSC wood is a good compromise, but consider alternatives like engineered and strand woven board. Kirei (www.kireiusa.com) uses strong, lightweight, durable, and environmentally friendly substitutes for furniture and cabinetry. Both their Kirei Board and Kirei Bamboo are recycled, come from renewable sources, and contain no formaldehyde in their adhesives. Using Kirei will also help you qualify for LEED points in your project.

Alabama Sawyer makes furniture, accessories, and cabinets using old-world craftsmanship with the finest joinery, built to last for generations. This

Modern Console by Sarreid Ltd.

knowledgeable firm coaches their clients in making eco-friendly choices to support the future of our global environment. This Greenopia-distinguished business works with walnut, cherry, maple, mesquite, elm, Pacific Coast maple, eucalyptus, and sycamore. They specify reclaimed lumber, backyard trees, and sustainable materials. Stains and finishes are water based and low VOC.

All of their pieces are made of 100 percent urban timber. These trees that have fallen due to natural attrition or development are generally a waste problem, headed right for the landfill or the chipper. The thing is—it's the most beautiful wood! Rather than being farmed to have uniform grain, the trees' natural environment affects the color and grain of the wood. This can be challenging in production. There is a reason that graded wood is better for mass production and construction, but for special pieces in a home or office, urban timber (and an expert craftsperson) ensures the piece is one of a kind, like the tree it came from and the person who buys it.

OUTDOOR FURNITURE

In addition to all of the health and environmental concerns related to any piece of furniture, outdoor pieces present their own unique challenges because

The Waverly Table from Alabama Sawyer (www.alasaw.com). (Photo by Cary Norton.)

The Alasaw Chair from Alabama Sawyer (www.alasaw.com). (Photo by Cary Norton.)

of the weather they are exposed to on a daily basis. It is important to select pieces that are extremely durable and able to last through multiple generations. The majority of outdoor furniture is made of virgin plastic material. Although it is water resistant, plastic has a tendency to break down in sunlight. Obviously, this isn't a good choice for multigenerational items.

Instead, choose materials that will hold up to the elements. Teak, cement, and bamboo have natural water-resistant properties and can withstand UV rays, which makes them perfect candidates for any high-moisture areas like poolside, bathroom, cabanas, and home spas. Composite materials made from wood and recycled high-density polyethylene are also good choices for long-lasting exterior furniture. When outdoor furniture is not in use, it is important to cover it or move it indoors.

Photos by Erika Bierman.

"The most sustainable way
is to not make things.
The second most sustainable
way is to make something
very useful to solve a
problem that hasn't been
solved."

—Thomas Sigsgaard

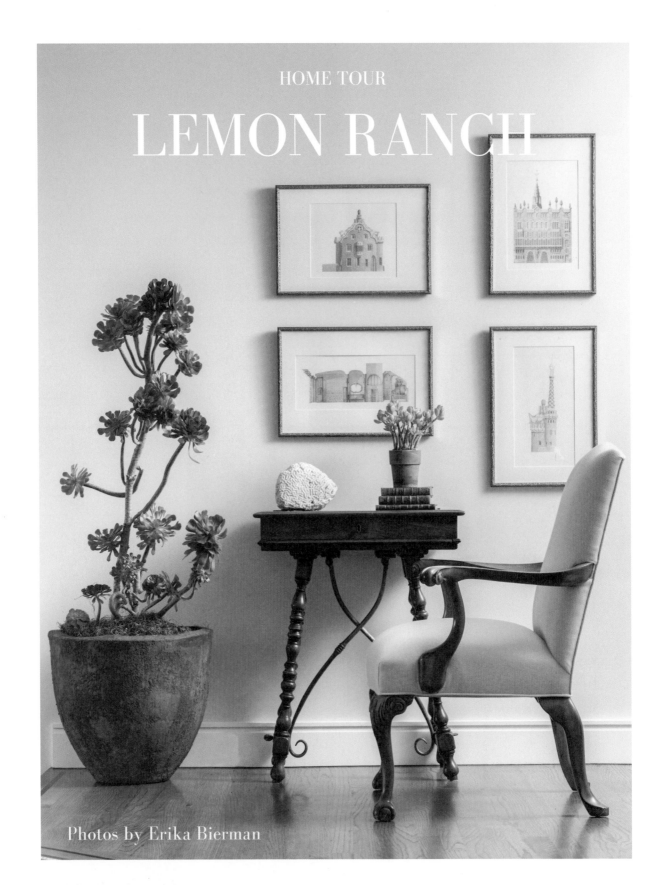

HOME TOUR

LEMON RANCH

Photos by Erika Bierman

WHAT MAKES THIS HOME GREEN?

We wanted to reach peak California Cool when we renovated this Lemon Ranch property in sunny Southern California, so that meant optimizing indoor-outdoor style! One of the best ways to do that is with outdoor fabrics. This home is filled with antique furniture recovered with Sunbrella indoor-outdoor fabrics. So the fabric will hold up as well as the frames!

Sunbrella's recycle program is incredible: They reuse their own leftovers to make new products; some are comprised of 50 percent postindustrial recycled materials. They operate with a zero-waste-to-landfill initiative. And all of the outdoor furniture frames are from our eco-pals at Teak Warehouse, whom we introduced above.

We updated the space with fresh paint and accessories and refinished and recovered most of the original antique furnishings. We also kept the original floors, cabinets, tiles, and counters.

The sofas were all custom creations from Gina Berschneider, an American manufacturer using all FSC wood frames. Her sofas are made to last for generations!

THE TEN COMMANDMENTS OF CALIFORNIA COOL INDOOR-OUTDOOR STYLE
What Is California Cool Style?

California Cool is light and breezy: it's citrus, salted air, and faint beach waves crashing in the distance. The aesthetic is minimal but still warm. It's not necessarily modern, but you wouldn't describe it as "timeless" either: that would feel too formal. It draws upon elements of contemporary coastal style with a little Southwest minimalism. Here are our Ten Commandments of California Cool Style:

1. **Keep Fabrics Clean and Organic.** Lean toward linens and other soft, breezy, organic fibers that resemble what you'd find outdoors, in nature, near the beach.

2. **Keep Palettes Light and/or Monochrome.** Having a variety of hues and various textures is important so your monochrome doesn't begin to look like you're lost in a snowstorm—including some browns and beiges in natural textures is a surefire way to make your monochromatic palette lean more toward spring/summer than winter whites.

3. **Warm Woods.** Wooden furnishings give this otherwise soft style a strong spine and still maintain its earthy, naturalistic atmosphere. By mixing and matching wood finishes, you can achieve various effects that all play within California Cool: for a vintage, lived-in, or more industrial look, perhaps you'll want some reclaimed pieces. In this home, we used the wood furnishings to add a sturdy, masculine touch and opted for clean, well-polished pieces.

4. **Focus on That Breezy Flow.** How easily air can flow from the outdoors through the space. When it comes to window treatments, that means lots of sheers! Throughout the Lemon Ranch project, low-e windows open for maximum airflow, seamlessly connecting the home's interior with the beautiful orchard outside.

Bernhardt furniture was used throughout the home. They are an incredible to-the-trade furniture manufacturer, prioritizing the ecological rights of their factories and suppliers. They ensure anyone they do business with prohibits child, prison, or slave labor and includes an environmentally sustainable initiative.

Xeriscaping the Backyard. The garden is largely drought resistant. Flowering succulents; dymondia ground cover; fruit groves; and bee, bird, and butterfly propagation complete this bountiful and low-maintenance outdoor space.

Choose a durable tile flooring that can carry you from indoors to out and doors and windows that allow a generous breeze.

5. **Outdoors as Luxe as the Inside.** Create outdoor spaces you can interact with as much as the inside. Carve out spaces to relax and bask in the sun. Include water features, edible gardens, maybe even a full kitchen? We love an outdoor dining room for entertaining al fresco!

6. **Keep Lines Relaxed.** "Relaxing" and "casual" are two of the first words that come to mind when you begin to describe California Cool style: this isn't a space for curling chesterfields and stiff, traditional upholstery. You should want to lounge in these spaces and spend some time: One measure of a good chair, after all, is how many different ways you can lounge in it and for how long.

7. **Rugs.** Rugs add pops of color and texture to an otherwise neutral color palette. We used Jaipur Rugs throughout this home—another organization with an incredible social mission, ensuring that all of their products are made in cruelty-free environments.

8. **Create Some Shade with a Cabana or Pergola.** Escape the sun, but still stay outdoors—get the best of both worlds by building a cabana or pergola. This is such an easy add-on that will elevate

your backyard design. You can really get creative with fabrics and colors and go wild with patterns and prints. With this pergola, we brought blues, yellows, and oranges and some plush lounge furniture into an otherwise beige space.

9. **Avoid the Kitschy Coastal Decor.** Lemon Ranch is a contemporary home mixed with antique furniture and well-traveled art. There are themes and textures that *hint* at coastal style, without hitting you over the head thematically. Gone are the days of adorning bookshelves in kitschy, dust-collecting seashell and lighthouse decor to achieve a nautical "theme." No more kitchen signs that remind you "You're at the Beach." That is, if anything, the opposite of California "Cool."

Think abstractly. Think about textures. At the beach, you have the contrast of the hot coarse sand with the silky palms and chilly ocean. Bring some of that indoors to continue the experience.

10. **Tailor Your Space.** It's trendy to associate the California Cool aesthetic with rattan and macramé, an abundance of indoor plants, and layers of jute rugs, but you don't need these elements to get the California Cool look. Instead, before overaccessorizing, take a tailored approach and add only what you need. Focus on the flow of the space from indoors to out, from one room to another, and focus on investment pieces: furnishings that will hold up to prolonged sun and salt air exposure and that will actually be utilized. Which brings us to our next section. . . .

Selamat Designs, a San Francisco–based home decor company, is known for their application of eco-friendly natural materials such as rattan, FSC-certified teak, and jute. Pictured: Selamat's new Art Deco Collection Stockholm Lounge Chair in black (available via www.shopcandelabra.com), Empire Chandelier (available via www.shopcandelabra.com), Empire Coffee Table (available via www.perigold.com), and Edith Side Table (available via www.perigold.com). (Photo courtesy of Selamat Designs, www.selamatdesigns.com.)

ACCESSORIES AND HOUSEWARES

Buy fewer accessories. We have a bad habit of buying too many things we really don't need to fill up houses that are too big. This has resulted in a huge debt problem and a vicious routine of carelessly consuming precious raw materials, polluting during production, packaging, and transportation, and incomprehensibly wasting valuable materials by adding these used-up products to the waste stream.

Not to mention, most accessories are made in countries where there is little or no regulation or regard for the health of workers, the consumer, or the environment. Granted, accessories can be useful and lovely additions to any interior, so choose them wisely! Pay attention to what they are made of; how they are made, packaged, and shipped; and how they can be recycled or last for many lifetimes.

There's No Such Thing as Free Shipping

Centralized online shopping sites like Amazon.com are both modern blessings and curses. They are undoubtedly useful for purchasing everything you need and prioritizing convenience above all else. Unfortunately; this results in a lot of shipping and packaging waste in the form of plastic wrap and cardboard, of which they are keenly aware.

Some ways to minimize waste is to use the service's option to have items ship together, rather than when they are soonest available. There are also online services like Loop (www.loopstore.com), whose mission it is to rival this by shipping everyday necessities in entirely recyclable packaging that you leave on your doorstep to be picked back up.

When it comes to shopping new accessories, we love finding lines that are aware of the environmental impact that designing, manufacturing, and shipping their products can have on the environment and do everything in their power to minimize them. Windy O'Connor accessories and art is one of those incredible companies!

They recognize that the average American disposes of 70 pounds of textiles per year, accounting for up to 15 percent of national landfill space. And that number is only growing. They do their best to repurpose every box that comes in their door to ship products.

They often cut them up and patch them to make the boxes for Windy's large original art pieces. They also reuse bubble wrap and any film plastic. They used to pack their pillows in film plastic for shipping but have switched to using more tape around the edges of the box for protection and layers of newsprint and tissue paper.

But perhaps the most sustainable thing they do is print the majority of their designs on natural fabrics like cotton and linen, and they support local printers. Their seamstress is around the corner from their office. They take their leftover velvet to their local seamstress to create beautiful "Good Vibes" bags that give you a good feeling about your day and the planet. They also donate linen and sateen to local quilters and to the Buddha Vocational Academy, an organization that teaches women and girls in Uganda marketable skills to start their own small business or how to compete in male-dominated fields. Ten percent of their bag sales are also donated to the Buddha Vocational Academy.

Although green accessories are better than their mainstream competitors, it's still not good to buy a bunch of knickknacks and toys that won't be used after the novelty is gone. Be selective when considering any accessory. Unless it truly serves a purpose, is a vision of inspiration, or will last a lifetime, don't buy it, even if it is green.

HOW TO DESIGN A SUSTAINABLE SHELFIE IN THREE STEPS

We believe the perfect sustainable shelfie shows you where you come from, where you've been, and where you're going. Don't use your shelf space to display mindless, cheap clutter imported to decor shops from overseas because it is trendy and "matches" the decor. Instead, create a sustainable shelfie by displaying what's important to you. Use it to showcase your memories in the form of antiques, photographs, and collections from your travels. Display books full of things you still want to learn about. Include accessories made of renewable resources and natural materials like pottery, or include some plants!

Step 1: Memories
Antiques
We love mixing old with new! And we love antiques because what could be more sustainable? Antiques add history and texture to a home, and their very existence proves they can withstand the test of time!

Collectables from Abroad
Because travel and global style is such an intrinsic part of our design aesthetic, we love to bring in antiques from near and far to remind us of where we've been and where we're going. We can't resist displaying a beautiful bargain buy from a Paris flea market or trinkets from Thailand!

Photographs
Of course, this one should go without saying—framed photographs of friends and family make the perfect sustainable shelfie accessory! Fill those shelves only with things that will make you smile when you walk by every day.

Art by Windy O'Connor.

"We can't just consume
our way to a more
sustainable world."

—Jennifer Nini

Step 2: Books

Shelves are for books, after all! Filmmaker John Waters famously advised against engaging with anyone whose bookshelves aren't full of books. And, while we've all gone digital and made great sustainable strides in doing so, there's still something about holding the physical media in your hand. The tactile experience of turning the paper pages and giving your eyes the rest they need from staring at screens all day is something we can't argue with, even from a sustainability perspective. Books, especially used books, look gorgeous on display shelves and obviously serve a functional purpose.

Step 3: Connecting with the Earth

Pottery

Pottery and other decor made from natural materials is always going to be your best bet if you have to buy new. Bonus points if it's a ceramic vase in which to display fresh-cut flowers from your garden!

Plants

Speaking of fresh-cut flowers . . . taking up shelf space with an indoor garden always gets the green light from us! A collection of succulents is on trend, sustainable, and incredibly easy to maintain.

Crystals

Raise your home's vibe with crystal accessories! Whether you just like them aesthetically or you're embracing your inner woo, crystals are beautiful natural accessories. Here are our favorite crystals to fill some shelf space with, along with the "properties" they are traditionally associated with:

- **Clear Quartz.** Known to be the most powerful of all crystals, clear quartz is a master healer and protector. Quartz is added to electronics, watches, cameras, cars' fuel lines, and acupuncture needles. It amplifies energy and all other crystals to the highest level.

- **Selenite.** This stone clears stagnant and unwanted energy. It guards against EMFs and increases inner peace and clarity.
- **Amethyst.** One of the most powerful and protective stones. It clears away negative energy and calms the mind.
- **Rose Quartz.** This is the stone of love and peace. It enhances all types of love: self-love, unconditional love, and compassion for others. It's known to raise positive energy and reduce stress.
- **Citrine.** The stone of business, personal power, creativity, and wealth. It's the stone of abundance. It promotes joy and releases negativity, fear, and anger.
- **Iron Pyrite.** This is the stone of wealth. Exuding high masculine energy, it blocks negative energy and pollutants, increases blood flow to the brain, and helps to stimulate the flow of ideas, inspiration, instinct, and big concepts. Fun fact about this stone: It grows naturally in perfect squares.
- **Tiger's Eye.** This stone of protection promotes rational and quick thinking and clear vision. It helps accomplish goals with clarity and focus and balances yin and yang energy. It assists with realistic manifestation rather than wishful thinking.
- **Lapis Lazuli.** This is the stone of peace, harmony, and clear communication. It's all about self-awareness, self-expression, and truth.

Everyone loves a beautifully curated shelfie photo in a glossy design magazine—but did you know most of those props are brought in by the photo stylist to amp up the glam specifically for the photoshoot? Once you're done designing and building and furnishing, stop before you go too crazy with accessorizing! *It's*

okay to have some empty shelf space. And if you're going to buy new, make sure it's sustainable. In the words of Marie Kondo, be sure it "sparks joy." If you're going to buy, buy sustainable.

RUGS

Area rugs are a more eco-friendly choice than wall-to-wall carpeting, and we'll explain why in chapter 4, "Surface Materials." When purchasing, select rugs that are made in environmentally and socially responsible ways, are created from renewable materials, or are antiques.

Lori Dennis sofa made of organic fabric, wool rug. (Media room by Lori Dennis. Photo by Ken Hayden.)

The austere, stone floor called out for something soft and sustainable to warm it up. Wool rugs, like the one seen in this photo, are naturally fire resistant and hold up to the toughest Super Bowl crowds. The sofa is made of Sensuede fabric which is made from recycled materials and spot cleans with a quick scrub of mild dish soap and water. Instead of turning up the heat, make throws accessible for a more cozy movie time.

Shopping Sustainable Rugs with a Social Mission

Jaipur (www.jaipurrugs.com) and **Surya Rugs** (www.surya.com) are both rug manufacturers with incredible product selections and are committed to social missions focused on ethical employment and fair wages. You can find their products on sites like Wayfair.com.

Pure (www.purerugs.com) features a sophisticated collection of cowhide rugs. All hides are from cows in the food industry. Their tanneries are certified as being low impact for the environment, and all rugs are biodegradable.

GoodWeave (www.goodweave.org) is an international foundation devoted to ending child labor by building schools and programs and creating opportunities for the nearly 300,000 children who are exploited in the rug industry. When you buy a rug from a RugMarkIndia.org vendor, you can be certain that no illegal child labor was used to produce it. The vendors supporting the foundation are some of the most well-known retailers in the world, and the styles range from modern to traditional.

Helios Carpets (www.helioscarpet.com) offers beautiful wool carpets with recycled and recyclable plastic cores. The company practices eco-friendly efforts in their plants, including gray wastewater, low-mercury light bulbs, green solvents for washing, and recycling yarn waste into a composite that is used for automobile mats. Excess wool is recycled into bionutrients for soil and all-natural carpet pads.

ACCESSORY LIGHTING

The importance of artificial lighting design is often overlooked in residential interiors. In a green home, the lighting plan is critical because of the amount of energy it can potentially waste. When an interior is well designed, natural light should flood the space during the day. With an abundance of natural light, you can space plan to take advantage of natural light so that artificial light only needs to be used at night. For example, place a desk or chair next to a window with lots of natural light. This will result in energy savings and a more pleasant daylight source.

For a successful lighting plan, there needs to be a good balance of ambient and task lighting. Indirect fluorescent lighting is a great eco-friendly, ambient source. Task lighting requires the lighting source to be directed precisely where it is needed. Frequently, recessed or under-counter lighting are used as task lighting sources. With innovations in lighting, these sources can now be fluorescent or LED instead of incandescent.

Most lamps that historically used incandescent bulbs can be replaced with compact fluorescent bulbs. The compact fluorescents last ten times as long and save considerable energy. To illustrate this point, place your hand near one of each that has been lit for ten minutes. The heat you feel coming off of the incandescent bulb is wasted energy.

Burned-out fluorescent lamps should always be disposed of properly, through facilities that capture the mercury and recycle the components. Don't throw them away in just any trash can.

LED bulbs are the most efficient bulbs available today. They consume a fraction of the energy that incandescent bulbs do, and because they are constantly evolving, the warm color is now very similar to that of incandescents. They do cost more but last thirty times as long as incandescents, creating a savings of $139 per bulb in utility costs. The good news is that LEDs are continuously becoming more affordable and available in accessory fixtures; they can be used with dimmers; and come in cool Edison-style bulbs.

Ten Bathroom Lighting Tips to Make Your Renovation Easy

Lighting in the bathroom has the potential to dramatically shift the aesthetics and mood of the space. Here are ten tips to help you get there:

1. Layers, Layers, Layers

We always like to stress the importance of lighting in layers! One overhead light isn't going to be sufficient or flattering—more on that in a minute. To break it down, think about lighting in three layers:

- **Ambient lighting.** This is going to be your general lighting that illuminates the entire room space. This is usually a chandelier or flush mount on the ceiling.
- **Task lighting.** As the name suggests, this is lighting that pinpoints specific "tasks." In the bathroom, this is going to be your vanity lighting.
- **Accent lighting.** This last layer is also focused light that illuminates dark corners or tight spaces. Think around the toilet.

2. Framing the Face

There's a reason the best baths all install sconces or pendant lighting at face level on either side of the vanity mirror. It's super flattering! Relying solely on overhead ambient lighting is going to cast shadows on your eyes and make you look tired and angry in the mirror. Generally sconces of pendants should sit on either side of the mirror about sixty-five inches from the floor and just a few inches from the edges of the outside of the mirror.

3. Wet-Rated Lighting for the Bathroom

Contrary to popular belief, not all the lights in the bath must be damp rated for wet spaces. Of course, there are a couple instances in which it is absolutely essential, namely as the main light above a bath or shower and ideally above the sink as well.

4. Wattage for Bathroom Lighting

Since baths are generally smaller spaces, you don't need a ton of wattage. About sixty watts should suffice. Perhaps even less in a small powder room or half bath.

5. Working with What You Have

In this Bel Air home, we wanted to use the lighting to complement the existing brass hardware (can you say '80s glam?! It's back, baby!) So we opted for these brass sconces from Lamps Plus that are just gorgeous!

6. Making a Statement

Think outside the box a little bit to make a statement with lighting in the bath! Bath bars and recessed lighting are not your only options. Think about adding a chandelier if you can, and consider the finishes.

7. Controllable Lighting in the Bath

Put as much as possible on dimmers! When you wake up in the morning and are getting ready, easing into your day, the last thing you want is to be blasted with unnatural light.

8. Chandeliers Versus Flush Mounts in the Bathroom

We love the look of a pretty crystal chandelier in a bathroom. It's classic and elegant. But if you have a low ceiling or it's not your style and you want something more streamlined, consider a flush mount over canned lighting.

9. LEDs or Not?

You'll just want to keep a few things in mind when shopping for bulbs: are they dimmable (most are), how bright are they, and what's the color temperature like? (The color temp is going to be a personal preference, but realizing that some bulbs are bluer or more golden than others should inform your decision.)

10. Lighting a Small Bathroom

You may be saying, What do I do if I only need to light a small powder room or my vanity isn't large enough to accommodate all of these different layers of light? Apply the same principles above to best suit the needs of your space. You can skip a step or two and still have the luxe space of your dreams. This is where a simple bath bar light can be incredibly helpful as both task and general light to illuminate the whole space or sconces that are flush against the walls. If your ceiling is too low for a chandelier, there are plenty of flush mounts that are water safe to install above a shower. You don't have to resort only to recessed lighting! It's time to get creative.

Our Most-Shopped Lighting Sources

Lamps Plus is a pioneer in putting LED bulbs in every lamp, even the exterior, which is so often overlooked!

Rocky Mountain Hardware (www.rockymountain hardware.com) earns five gold stars from us. They are based in Idaho, and they have a new line of LED indoor lighting that is gorgeous and made from 90 percent recycled metal. Using their light fixtures can help you to qualify for two points toward LEED certification. Their headquarters are LEED Gold certified.

Stray Dog Designs (www.straydogdesigns.com) is an HGTV Greenhouse vendor with a collection of some of the most unique lamps and adorable accessory lamps you'll ever see, featuring shapes and colors nowhere else to be found. The products are handmade with recycled materials by local artisans in San Miguel de Allende, high in central Mexico's mountainous desert, a mecca for tin products. The company is a big supporter of paying local artisans and workers fair wages, helping stray animals, and modeling green social behavior. Every time you buy a Stray Dog Design product, they donate a portion of the profit to feed hungry children, shelter homeless families, and create loving homes for stray animals. This is one accessory you can own and feel really good about.

AUTOMATED LIGHTING SYSTEMS

Using dimmers, timers, and motion detectors in conjunction with artificial light sources reduces energy loads in the home. Dimmers should be installed in dining, bedroom, living room, and hallways. Sensors should be placed in bathrooms, pantries, closets, hallways, and exterior lights.

Timers work well with exterior lighting. Whole house automated systems can combine all of these functions with a centralized controller that runs programmable zones. Syncing these systems with phone, internet, and security systems provides the most efficient energy use and eliminates waste.

Lutron Electronics is a world leader in residential lighting control systems and one of our firm's go-tos. The company offers a wide selection of light dimmers, whole-home-dimming systems, and motorized window treatments. **Control4** is an affordable alternative. It's an efficient, scalable system and alerts you via email in the event of a water leak, fire, or security breach. With access screens that can be viewed throughout the home or via the internet, Control4 provides homeowners peace of mind while respecting the planet. Brochures are printed on recycled materials.

SOY VEGETABLE CANDLES VERSUS PETROLEUM PARAFFIN CANDLES

When you think of candlelight, relaxing, spa-like environments come to mind. Candlelight can be a soothing and wonderful way to create a mood, but most candles are toxic when they're burned, releasing harmful chemicals into the air. Most candles are made from petroleum by-products and contain benzene and toluene, both known carcinogens. Artificially scented candles may contain phthalates. Once these paraffin candles are burned, they release these chemicals and add to indoor air pollution.

Soy or beeswax candles burn longer and cleaner. Soy wax spills are easier to clean compared to paraffin candle wax, which stains fabric and carpets. Soy candles also act as a diffuser because they burn slower, allowing for a cooler flame near the oil. When the oil is not burned, it diffuses around the room more evenly.

And they're not necessarily more expensive: Mrs. Meyer's candles, for example, retail at around $10 and fit the bill. Some of our other favorite, slightly higher-end lines include MALIN+GOETZ and Le Labo. (These are Courtney's personal favorite candles to give as host gifts. She gives them all the time and is always open to receiving them! *hint hint*)

The Olive Branch chandelier from Stray Dog Designs is a stunning piece handcrafted from iron and recycled paper in their San Miguel de Allende workshop. It is finished with zero-VOC and low-odor paint, which is safe for their artisans and the environment. (Photo by Graham Yelton.)

3

FABRICS AND WINDOW TREATMENTS

The choices in eco-friendly fabrics have really expanded in the last twenty years. The variety of textures, patterns, and colors now rivals that of mainstream fabrics due to advances in green manufacturing and raw material sourcing. But at a time when every company is calling their product eco-friendly or green, how can we make the best choices? There are degrees of how sustainable a fabric is and, in addition to your own research, labels and organizations like Global Organic Textile Standards (GOTS), Greenguard, and Green Seal can help you make that determination. Ask yourself the questions below when researching fabric for your projects.

Are the fabric and its manufacturing process free of harmful chemicals? Any of two thousand chemicals can be used during the manufacturing process, leaving residual amounts in the fabrics that can leach into the water supply, pollute the air, and be absorbed by our skin. Formaldehyde, for example, is frequently used in conventional manufacturing to help cloth retain its uniformity (won't bunch) and size (won't shrink). This process is toxic not only to the environment and consumers but also to the employees who handle the chemical for forty hours every week. Organic fabric manufacturers are giving the consumer an option to purchase textiles without the chemical additives.

Is it from a renewable resource? If it's a synthetic fiber, is it 100 percent recyclable and made from recycled-content material? Is it an antique?

When the fiber comes from an animal, has it been purchased from a farm that is free range and doesn't practice animal cruelty?

How long will the fabric be usable before it shows signs of wear and needs to be replaced? The more durable a fabric is, the longer it will last. Long-lasting fabric is more environmentally friendly than that which must be replaced often. Treatments like Nanotex, an environmentally friendly permanent, stain-repellent finish, make fabrics easy to clean and able to withstand years of use.

Is the fabric biodegradable? Is there an alternative option to becoming part of the waste stream at the end of its useful life? As a side note here, consider donating excess fabric or worn-out fabric to design schools. They are in constant need of fabrics for projects. Imagine your old bedspread could be an inspiration in Armani's line one day. And you kept the fabric out of the trash.

Fabrics are made from plant fibers, animal fibers, and synthetic fibers. We've all seen the ads touting material as "all natural." While the word has a wholesome ring to it, it certainly doesn't mean it's nontoxic, healthy, or a good choice. Reviewing where the fibers come from helps you to make informed decisions about the appropriate types of fabric to use in your interior or exterior spaces.

PLANT FIBERS 101
Now let's get into the weeds of it! (Pun intended.) Here's the section where we'll really break down the plant fibers that comprise our fabrics.

Cotton
When you see a label saying a fabric is "natural cotton," you may think it's a green choice. The truth is

Using antique fabrics is yet another way to reduce your carbon footprint. These Nathan Turner throw pillow and suzani are made from fabric that is over a hundred years old. In this old-world courtyard, they were the perfect finishing touch to soften the sea of stone. (Courtyard by Lori Dennis. Photo by Ken Hayden.)

that conventional cotton, although a small percentage of the world's agricultural crops, uses 25 percent of the world's pesticides. Every pound of cotton that is grown uses a third of a pound of pesticide, which pollutes the groundwater in many countries.

On the other hand, organic cotton is a green fiber. Never genetically modified, it doesn't use poisonous chemicals found in polluting pesticides, herbicides, and fertilizers. Instead, eco-friendly techniques like crop rotation and introduction of natural predators are used in organic cotton cultivation. All organic cotton farmers must meet GOTS guidelines during cultivation and production. Organic certification also includes annual inspections of land and crops by reputable certifying organizations.

Linen

Linen comes from the flax plant. Although growing flax creates far less pollution than cotton cultivation, the growing of flax requires mass quantities of herbicides, as flax is not competitive with weeds. The conventional growing of flax pollutes water through a process called "retting," which separates the fiber from the stalk by rotting it away. This process creates butyric acid, methane, and hydrogen sulfide, which has a rotten smell.

If the water is not treated before its disposal, it creates pollution in waterways. Organic flax cultivation requires manual weeding and rotation of crops to fight off weeds and potential disease. Organic producers of flax "artificially ret" the flax, and this method results in no toxic wastewater. With its high moisture absorbency, high heat conductivity, and excellent abrasion resistance, linen (flax) is an excellent choice for upholstery.

Bamboo

Often called a sustainable wonder plant, bamboo is a renewable fiber that has natural antibacterial qualities. The plants grow quickly, don't require pesticides, absorb four times the CO_2 that other plants do, and release 35 percent more oxygen.

Nettle

Nettle, a common weed, has been called the next bamboo. Plants grow quickly without the use of pesticides. They are mowed and dried once per year and require replanting only once every fifteen years. The fabric hasn't been marketed very well but is a cost-competitive alternative to cotton.

Hemp

Hemp is an extremely durable fabric that naturally resists mold and UV light, and can be machine washed. It's a great choice for a shower curtain, drapery, or slip-covered furniture. It grows fast in any kind of climate, uses little water, does not exhaust the soil, and requires no pesticides or herbicides. It is considered by many as the most versatile and sustainable plant on the earth because of its many uses: biofuels, paper, fabrics, ropes, building material, skin care products, and even food.

Seacell

Seacell fabric is synthetic cellulose fabric made out of wood pulp fiber (lyocell) and seaweed. The theory is that your skin will absorb the nutrients from seaweed (which combats cellulite), so bedding made of seacell fabric is a desirable, detoxing option.

Soy Fiber

Soy fiber is made from the waste product of soybeans. Organic cultivation does not require any bleach or toxins when soy is processed into fibers for fabric. Soy fiber fabric is called vegetarian cashmere because it is extremely soft. The fabric is resistant to UV rays and naturally antibacterial.

Lyocell

Lyocell is a fiber made from wood pulp cellulose. It is strong, soft, naturally wrinkle resistant, and absorbent. It drapes well, which makes it an ideal choice for fabric drapery treatments.

Bark Cloth

Made from the bark of mutuba trees, bark cloth is a 100 percent biodegradable, sustainable material. Textures range from fleece to leatherlike, and it can be molded.

ANIMAL FIBERS

If you're going to use any of these animal fibers, you want to make sure the supplier is shearing the animals in a humane way. You're likely going to pay more for the fibers of animals that are treated with concern, but that's the cost trade-off for being green, and we say it's well worth it.

Wool

Made from sheep hair, wool is renewable, biodegradable, and durable, yet soft. The fabric is wrinkle resistant and retains shape well. Wool has natural insulative properties, which makes it good for bedding and drapery.

Cashmere

Cashmere comes from the hair of Kashmir goats. The hair is collected every spring and hand woven into a fine, soft fabric. Because the fiber is so delicate, resulting in the need to handle collection, manufacturing, and processing by hand, cashmere is a sustainable and energy-efficient fabric.

Alpaca

Alpaca fiber is considered one of the best fabrics because it is as soft as cashmere, warmer than wool, more durable than cotton, and is naturally hypoallergenic due to the absence of lanolin. The material does not mat or pill and is naturally stain and wrinkle resistant. The material is so strong that three-thousand-year-old intact pieces have been found in the Peruvian mountains.

Camel Hair

Also called camel wool, this fabric has similar characteristics to wool and cashmere. It is collected as camels naturally shed in the late spring. The fabric has a rich, well, camel color, which doesn't need to be dyed. Its adaptable humidity qualities that change with air's moisture content make it perfect for bedding and upholstery. It also becomes softer every time it is washed.

Leather

Organic leather sounds like an oxymoron. However, the leather used is actually a by-product of cows that were raised for their meat. The hides come from animals that are organically fed and humanely treated. The conventional technique used to tan leather involves chrome and other heavy metals that emit toxic fumes and contaminate water and air. During an organic tanning process, natural plant matter is used to cure the leather rather than toxic chemicals.

Silk

Silk comes from the unwound fiber of silkworm cocoons. It is a renewable, biodegradable, durable fabric. Conventional silk kills the moth by steaming it to death so farmers can obtain an intact cocoon with longer fibers. Organic silk farming allows the moth to leave the cocoon and then collects them for processing. This method results in much shorter fibers (that the moth has broken through) resulting in lower yield and higher-priced silk.

SYNTHETIC FABRICS

Although many synthetic fabrics are made from petroleum-based products, they can still be considered green. Some synthetic fabrics are spun from recycled pre and postconsumer materials, like plastic bottles and waste from industrial production. This diverts waste from landfills and converts it into useful raw materials. Some of these recycled-content fabrics are extremely durable and last many lifetimes. Even more sustainable are fabrics created from recycled waste, which can be recycled into new raw materials when their life span is over. In the recent past, synthetic fabrics used in contract applications looked commercial. Innovations in technology and boutique hotel popularity, however, have transformed the look of these fabrics into suitable styles for residential interiors. These types of synthetics are easily cleaned, fire resistant, contain recycled and recyclable content, and look fabulous.

The factories that manufacture these eco-friendly materials practice environmental responsibility in their factories and when shipping. Many follow strict GOTS guidelines, use low-impact ink, recycle waste into usable materials, test for indoor air quality, follow fair trade standards, and pay living wages.

Sensuede is a synthetic fiber made of recycled materials. We love using it when upholstering in light colors because it's easy to keep clean. We did a lot of this in our Bond at the Beach project that you'll see throughout the home tour. No need to panic when dirty hands touch this sofa; you simply spot clean with a cotton towel soaked in mild dish soap and water. Voilà, the light-colored sofa is as good as new.

From drapery to bedding to furniture, fabric makes up a huge part of our interior design budgets. Thankfully, eco-friendly choices are becoming abundant and are some of the finest looking sold today.

How to Make Your Monochromatic Room Not Look Like a Snowstorm

Monochromatic rooms are clean, elegant, and can be a great blank canvas for those who enjoy changing up their accent decor from time to time. White on white is a popular trend among fans of chic minimalism and those who favor that "California Cool" aesthetic that's becoming popular even outside of Southern California. But when done incorrectly, it can make a space look like a snowstorm!

Choosing a Monochromatic Color Palette

Monochromatic doesn't always have to mean shades of gray! It can be tones of any color you choose. Tone-on-tone blue, for example, is a common design choice for monochromatic rooms for its elegant richness. But how do you choose a base color? How do you choose complementary shades? First, start with some basic color terminology that's important in developing your own monochromatic palette:

- Color/Hue: Refers to how much light reflected by the object
- Color Value: Refers to a color's degree of brightness
- Tint: Refers to a color's value after white has been added
- Shade: Refers to a color when black has been added
- Tone: Refers to the color's value after gray has been added

For a comfortably layered look, you'll want a palette comprised of a variety of color values—that will give your space that designer touch you see on the glossy pages of your favorite design magazines and prevent the room from looking flattened out. Another good place to start is by considering the colors that are already in the space: The flooring (Is it a dark wood, for example? That might be a good base color to start with!), or what do you see just outside the windows? (Is it mostly blue sky? Lots of greenery?), and so forth.

Choosing Monochromatic Textiles

You'll want to select fabrics that are easy to maintain because up against other fabrics of the same color, they're more likely to show blemishes and discoloration, especially in a lighter, brighter monochromatic palette. Common choices for easily maintained sofa fabrics, for example, include:

- Cotton
- Linen (Design tip: Both cotton and linen might snag or pill over time, so you might want to opt for something stronger or invest in a higher-end cotton or linen.)
- Synthetic microfiber (While this may not be the most environmentally sound option, it does have its benefits: for example, synthetic microfiber can be made to look like other materials.)
- Wool
- Leather (Wool and leather are both great, sleek, heavy-duty options!)

Accenting Monochromatic Rooms with Patterns, Scale, and Shine!

Add depth and texture to your monochromatic space by including a vast array of patterns. We've written about how fearful some people can be of color in their homes, and playing with loud prints that fit into your monochromatic palette can be a fun alternative. Some options to consider:

- Stripes and dots: Consider the iconic Kate Spade look in which she layers black and white stripes against black and white polka dots: dots and stripes are a great place to start, whatever your palette might be.
- Scale: After choosing patterns, you can also play with scale (smaller polka dots on larger, thicker stripes, for example).
- Mixed metals: In a monochromatic space, you should pay extra attention to choosing hardware and furniture frames, as they'll stand out against your palette and provide a great design opportunity. A great way to accent a monochromatic space and add depth is with something shiny, and one of the best ways to do that is with a mix of metals in hardware and furniture frames.

(A mixture of gold and silver is super popular right now in living spaces and can work for a variety of design styles from boho chic to high glamour!)

WHERE WE SHOP SUSTAINABLE FABRICS

Harmony Art (www.harmonyart.com) has some very inexpensive, double-wide, biodegradable organic textiles. The designs are pretty trippy, and we're into that. They're also GOTS compliant.

Sensuede (www.sensuede.com) is the first luxury faux suede fabric that's eco-friendly. Made entirely from recycled plastic bottles and polyester fibers, Sensuede is durable and luxurious. The Silky and Flannel Suede lines come in a wide variety of colors.

SmithHönig (www.smithhonig.com) Founded by Kelli Smith and Melanie Hönig, the brand focuses on all things boho luxe, vintage, vegan, and socially aware. The line includes original electric patterned fabrics and one-of-a-kind textiles, pillows, tassels, and decor.

OUTDOOR

Outdoor fabrics have come such a long way in terms of aesthetics. Now many of them are just as beautiful as indoor fabrics. Whenever possible, we try to use them for upholstery because they are ultradurable and very resistant to fading, wear, and tear. Many of these fabrics can be cleaned in a washing machine, so there is no need for dry cleaning slipcovers. It also makes your decorating transition from indoor to outdoor rooms seamless. Many outdoor fabrics come in luxurious velvets and sheers with coordinating tassels and trim.

Sunbrella (www.sunbrella.com) makes some of our favorite fabrics. We've used them for awnings, outdoor drapery, outdoor throws, and all types of upholstery, indoors and out! The company offers recycling for its customers using pre and postconsumer waste and repurposing it into a variety of recycled products. During

Girl's room at the midcentury home of SmithHönig cofounder and designer Kellie Smith features a draped toile daybed, dark walls and floors, and SmithHönig's repurposed textile pillows. On the floor, vegan travel bags from SmithHönig. (Photo by M. Hönig.)

The Venetian-inspired dining room in SmithHönig cofounder Melanie Hönig's home includes a hand-painted mural on plaster, artwork by Italian painter Alberto Le Tasso, and a handmade Bedouin camel tassel adorning the bar. Proceeds from sales of the Bedouin tassels benefit a women's empowerment center, founded by villagers in the Negev Desert. (Photo by M. Hönig.)

Indoor and outdoor living can be an organic experience in more ways than one. Durable Sunbrella fabric makes this bathroom ottoman water repellent and easy to clean. Makeup hands and wet bottoms are welcome here! (Photo by Erika Bierman.)

manufacturing, the company dramatically reduces water and energy consumption and avoids harmful effluents in the dyeing process. Sunbrella is Greenguard certified for indoor air quality. Awnings are a large part of Sunbrella's business, and by virtue of their design intent of reducing solar rays' intrusion into buildings, they help eliminate 10 to 40 percent of cooling needs.

Crypton (www.crypton.com) performance fabrics are taking over! This company started producing low-maintenance fabrics for assisted-living centers for which you really didn't even need soap or cleaning products to wipe up spills, and they've expanded their reach tenfold with bright, bold patterns and prints utilizing the same performance technology. Their new Nomad collection speaks to the maximalism trend we're seeing emerge all over the place. It's all about color, print, and chintz!

STAIN GUARDS

Prolonging fabric life by reducing the amount of stains and fading that may occur is a green practice, but many stain guards on the market are highly toxic. You can smell the VOC off-gassing for months. While it is a good idea to extend the life of fabric by protecting it with a stain guard, it is imperative to select a nontoxic, environmentally friendly solution.

One of our favorites is Ultra-Guard (www.ultra-guard.com). It's nontoxic and hypoallergenic. It repels both oil- and water-based stains and contains ultraviolet inhibitors to reduce fading. Another excellent selection is 303 Fabric Guard (www.sailrite.com), endorsed by Sunbrella for protection against mildew-, oil-, and water-based stains and fading from the sun. The product is nontoxic and odorless when it dries.

WINDOW TREATMENTS

Window treatments are green by design—they are intended to help control the amount of heat gain or loss through windows. Their insulating and light-blocking properties help reduce heating and cooling energy loads. Their materials should consist of renewable, nontoxic fibers that do not emit harmful VOCs. Some imported plastic and PVC blinds have been found to break down in ultraviolet light and produce toxic dust and have been known to off-gas for their entire lifespan. They should not be specified in a green home.

Window treatments must be cleverly designed to be able to utilize the natural power of solar energy to light a room but strong enough to withstand its deteriorating effects. Successful designs will allow natural light in interiors while still providing privacy.

When an occupant in the home is an allergy or asthma sufferer, blinds that can be regularly vacuumed are a better choice than fabric treatments. If you customize window treatments with a local fabricator, be sure to supply them with or specify sustainable fabric.

Closing the curtains can save an average of 25 percent on heat in the winter and air-conditioning in the summer. Make your carbon footprint even lighter by using an organic fabric like the one shown on page 86. When privacy is needed, but you want to take advantage of natural light, consider a sheer top and opaque bottom.

WHAT MAKES THIS HOME GREEN?

The goal here was to keep intact as much of the structure, molding, flooring, and cabinetry—just

Photo by Mark Tanner.

Photo by Erika Bierman.

HOME TOUR

LAKE SHERWOOD

Photos by Mark Tanner

refurbish everything so it was good as new! What we kept: The old door handles and faucets were replated; the originals from the '80s are totally back in style but needed a little refresher.

All the paints were low VOC. In the bathrooms and kitchens, cabinets were made new by adding a backsplash. We painted the cabinets and molding throughout the home with fresh new colors. In the bathrooms, we also kept the existing tile, and we retained the existing kitchen counters. There was no need to trash perfectly good material and replace with new natural stone that would have to come out of a quarry and be transplanted. And luckily, the appliances in place were already long lasting and energy efficient!

We tried reusing existing furniture as much as possible. The rugs throughout the home are from Jaipur, a socially responsible company that prioritizes

ethical working conditions and gives back to the local communities. The Jaipur Rugs Foundation (JRF) trains weavers in areas with no viable work within their immediate area. These areas are selected on the basis of a survey by the government of India identifying the most economically stunted geographies in the country.

What was new: We replaced with all custom window treatments to allow in natural light and a chandelier with LED fixtures.

YOUR GUIDE TO WINDOW TREATMENTS 101

Depending on your home's style and what region you live in, think of window treatments as the sunglasses or scarves of your home—both stylish accessories that serve a real, protective purpose. As designers, we get asked a lot of questions about window treatments, such as "How necessary are window treatments?" and "When do you decide to go without them?" The truth is draperies serve a number of functions beyond their aesthetics and are, indeed, necessary in a number of circumstances. We work with the Heritage Draperies workroom here in Los Angeles

on all of our projects to help us customize drapery for our clients. Here are just a few of the functions draperies serve:

- Draperies protect furniture, floors, rugs, and carpet from harmful UV rays.
- Drapes improve your home's energy efficiency by insulating interiors from summer heat and winter cold.
- They also allow you better light control for creating mood and atmosphere. This can be the difference between a room you use or don't during a blindingly bright afternoon glare.
- Drapes offer privacy; that's a given.
- They can also control acoustics for soundproofing. Along with your rugs, drapes can be essential for noise absorption in particularly echoey spaces.

Those are the practical functions; here are some of the ways drapes and shades serve a space aesthetically:

- Draperies define the characteristics of a room by adding individual style and beauty through an array of color, pattern, and texture.
- They add softness, elegance, and handcrafted luxury. Shrouding the space in softness also makes it feel more comfortable—like a big hug from your window sweaters.
- Window treatments also enhance architectural details—you invested in beautiful crown molding or ceiling beams and a chandelier; drapes are a great way to draw the eye upward to them.
- Sometimes window treatments can correct the structural flaws of windows, walls, ceilings, and floors by applying proper scale, proportion, or symmetry.

What Materials?

Window treatments are a fun area where you can get creative with a lot of fabric options. You can soften and set the mood with a large piece of fabric that adds character and texture: Silky smooth in the bedroom, maybe?

Or perhaps it's a light, breezy linen in the sunroom? Heavier fabrics lined to black out light contrast beautifully when layered in front of lace curtains. Consider how much sun exposure they're going to get to choose durable fabrics that won't fade.

How Much Do Custom Window Treatments Cost?

The costs are all over the place and vary depending on a few elements:

- Size of window.
- Materials of window treatments. Think: Does it have trim or decorative elements? (Decorative tassels or trims can add cost). Is it a full heavy drapery? Or a lighter drapery without lining—billowing sheers letting light through? Or are your drapes lined? Are they lined to black out all light? The fabric itself could be $5 per yard or $250 per yard, which will really affect pricing.
- Type of window treatment and height. Are there valance treatments? Or swags? Do your drapes hang all the way from the ceiling, or do they just brush the top of the window? How much fabric will obviously alter the price as well. Which brings us to our next point. . . . How do you determine how long your drapes *should* be?

How Long and Wide Should Drapes Be? And How Should Window Treatments Be Installed?

There are standard window treatment sizes (these measure 63 to 144 inches long; widths should be about 2.5 times the window width), but depending

on the effect you're hoping to achieve in your space, you may need something custom:

- In a grand dining or formal living room, for example, you may want to emphasize height by hanging drapes from a very high ceiling all the way to the floor.
- If you have custom-sized windows, perhaps a floor-to-ceiling window, you'll also require something custom, especially if they wrap or are particularly wide.
- As a rule of thumb, you'll want to measure from the floor to where to you want to hang the rod, and it's always better to round up to the nearest inch—you'll likely want to hit the floor or nearly brush up to it. Anything shorter will probably look just a little bit . . . off.

The Devil Is in the Details . . .

You've selected the fabric and correct size for your window treatments, but hold on—you're not quite done yet! There are a number of little details that will actually affect the overall aesthetic of how your drape looks once it's hung:

- The top part of a curtain is known as the "heading," and you have a lot of customization here that is going to affect how the drape hangs: hooks connected to the top of the curtain, for example, allow for it to lie flat and be easily manipulated open or closed; a pocket in the top of the curtain for the rod, by contrast, creates a nice gathered look but makes opening and closing trickier.
- Speaking of which, don't forget about rods, finials, and tiebacks! Tiebacks can be in the form of hardware hooks that connect to the wall and usually match the hardware used for the rods. Tiebacks can also be a rope or linen trim that matches

the style and palette of the window treatment. Finials (those little things at the ends of the rods) are a great way to continue a motif, whether it's a particular shape or object or a colored crystal to match the chandelier.

Natural Grass Shades

Besides being renewable resources that may only take a few months to replenish themselves, natural fibers in window shades have other advantages. They are appropriate for any style interior. Plants such as flax and hemp are durable and have a high resistance to ultraviolet rays. Many natural fibers, like bamboo, have antimicrobial properties that make them extremely resistant to mold. Some fibers, like flax, have a natural wax that makes a beautiful sheen on the window treatment material.

Earthshade products (www.earthshade.com) are available in ten styles, and all their patterns have insulating and sun shading properties. For colder climates, they offer a hemp insulation liner. No pesticides are used in their crops, and coloration is achieved by natural techniques like sun bleaching or oven baking. All shades are available in custom sizes, with optional automation systems and lifetime warranties.

Wood Blinds

Wood blinds can be a desirable choice for a green interior because they are easy to clean, long lasting, and do a good job of blocking out ultraviolet rays. Make sure they made of are FSC certified, composite, or faux wood.

Anyone wanting to recycle old blinds or shades can drop them off at any of the one hundred plus Blinds to Go (www.blindstogo.com) locations throughout the country. Blinds to Go will bring them to a local recycling center.

4

SURFACE MATERIALS

These days, sustainable surface materials are easily found and come in a wide variety of attractive styles. The price is often right in line with conventional materials, and the look is indistinguishable. Selecting sustainable products, however, makes a vast improvement in the effects these products have on environmental and human health.

The reduction or elimination of pollutants significantly improves air quality for both indoor and outdoor environments. This is especially important for people who suffer the effects of sick building syndrome. Conservation of energy also reduces climate change and acid rain, greatly improving our planet's ability to sustain life.

Using green materials aids in water conservation and waste reduction, and reuse and recycling materials helps to preserve precious natural resources. But in order for recycling to make economic sense, consumers will need to purchase materials made with recycled content. Purchasing surface materials made of recycled materials helps to fuel this need.

Equally important, buying green materials ensures that laborers are not exposed to toxins and exploitation. It certainly feels right to know that the people who produce the materials that make our interiors shine are not being treated unfairly.

When selecting materials, it is also important to keep their future maintenance requirements in mind. For example, choosing smooth surface materials will make them easier to clean than textured ones, thereby using less time, less energy, and fewer cleaning products. This is especially true of bathroom and kitchen walls, which tend to get dirtier than any other walls in the home. Having washable surfaces, like tile or

semigloss paint, helps to prevent stains and extends the life of these areas.

FLOORING

Wood Flooring

Wood is one of the most durable flooring materials. Often a wood floor that looks like it's past its prime simply needs to be refinished. Consider this possibility before rushing out to buy something new or reclaimed.

Once floors are refurbished, they may be more beautiful and durable than anything you can purchase. If you decide to take this route, seal the rest of the house off from the area that is being refinished so wood dust particles, which likely contain toxins, are not spread throughout the home. Depending on how old the floors are, there may well be lead paint and other highly toxic substances that will be kicked up into the air and can make a homeowner extremely sick. Use low-VOC, water-based products for the new applications.

If a new or reclaimed wood floor is going to be installed, start with a green subfloor and products that have been FSC certified and contain no formaldehyde. They will emit lower levels of unhealthy chemicals. (Nontoxic subflooring is not always easy to locate and can be substantially higher-priced than conventional subfloor materials.)

Hardwood floors are so durable that they can sometimes last longer than their original homes. Older wood floors are often high-quality and beautiful. Because buildings use an extraordinary amount of new lumber, some green lumber companies specialize in

Photo by Mark Tanner.

finding reclaimed or used wood. Reusing old wood is a good green approach to reducing the amount of new lumber needed in a home. When using reclaimed lumber, make sure to instruct your installer to finish the reclaimed wood with environmentally friendly stains and finishes. As a last resort, select new lumber for wood flooring. When doing so, it is imperative that the wood is from managed forests and be FSC certified.

Flooring choices heavily impact your design direction. Whether you are going for casual, beachy chic, or a sophisticated zen vibe, you can incorporate a sustainable floor material. In this entry, hand-scooped bamboo planks were impregnated with an espresso color that will hold up to busy foot traffic. Bamboo is a grass that regrows to full maturity much quicker than hardwood. It's generally pretty inexpensive too.

The kitchen in this Southern California beach house is exposed to sand, sea air (i.e., salt), and lots of guests who want to enjoy the Pacific Ocean. It was mandatory to have a low-maintenance, highly durable surface in the home. Our solution was to use reclaimed bleacher planks from a nearby high school. The homeowners and many of their guests actually sat on these very same bleachers when attending high school basketball games. It makes for a fun story and a floor that has clearly proven it can stand the test of time.

What's the difference between actual wood flooring and engineered veneer? Stone versus porcelain? What type of flooring is best for pets and children? How much maintenance is necessary? Let's sort it all out. Here are the pros and cons of popular flooring materials and our answers to your frequently asked questions about flooring:

FAQs: Wood Flooring Versus Porcelain Tile

Q. Why Is Wood Flooring So Popular?

Wood flooring is classic, enduring, strong. It lasts a long time, and you can sand it down a few times so it will look like new. It gives a home a warm, lived-in feel. And you can really get creative with the installation design: herringbone, inlays and parquet, and other fancy applications, or you can opt for a more traditional installation for a rustic and down-to-earth feel. We're in a light wood trend right now, which has a much brighter, casual modern feel than the heavy darker rich wood floorings of the past.

Q. What If Wood Flooring Is Outside My Budget? Is There an Inexpensive Alternative?

If you like the look of wood but feel it may be outside your budget, look toward wood-like porcelain tile. It's less expensive but looks great and keeps the home cool in the summer. It's also a great selection because you can install radiant heat below.

Another option is engineered hardwood veneer. It's also less expensive and looks great. It has a thinner top layer than solid hardwood. The downside to consider is that it might be harder than hardwood floor because of the glue needed to keep the plies together. So get ready to invest in a lot of plush area rugs!

Vinyl is also an affordable look that is easily maintained and can resemble wood. Because it's so hygienic, you'll see it used in a lot of hospitals, restaurants, and hospitality public spaces.

Q. How Different Will Wood-Like Porcelain Tile Look from Actual Wood?

It can vary, but here is a pro design tip to get around that issue: match the grout to the tile color so it blends and isn't obvious that it's not wood. This is great because it can continue throughout the house in a seamless, continuous way from home into wet-surface areas like kitchens and bathrooms.

Q. In What Rooms Should I Install Wood Flooring? Any I Should Avoid?

Wood is beautiful in just about every interior space, but in bathrooms and laundry rooms or other spaces that involve moisture like indoor-outdoor spaces, for example, you might actually want to opt for wood-like porcelain, which is both heat and stain resistant, so you don't have to worry about flooding or any water damage. Because it's comprised of clays and minerals fired at extremely high temperatures, it's an incredibly durable material, making it one of *the* best choices for flooring, as opposed to ceramic, which is not going to hold up as well.

FAQs: Stone Versus Porcelain Tile Flooring

Q. What Are the Benefits of Stone Tile?

Stone is classic, resistant, and natural. Though it comes at a higher price, it lasts forever. With stone, you have a lot of creative freedom to design borders, install herringbone, diagonal, or large scale—you can even craft smaller architectural details, which we love!

Q. If Real Stone Is Outside My Price Point, What Is an Alternative?

Ceramic and porcelain tile are both cost-efficient alternatives to actual stone tile. The ceramic manu-facturing process has come a long way so that it looks closer to real stone, rather than a pixelated picture. Porcelain is extremely strong and is a great alterna-tive to stone. It comes in large slabs like stone, for a modern application.

Q. What Are the Benefits of Concrete Flooring?

Concrete tile is so fun and makes a real WOW moment in color and design! It's among the most durable materials and can be entirely customized to fit your specifications. It's heat and scratch resistant, capturing and releasing the heat in your home for optimal comfort.

Q. What Type of Flooring Should I Avoid Altogether?

We rarely recommend carpeting because it's a total dust and dirt collector. Carpet can be toxic in its application and material, not to mention it's more expensive and difficult to maintain. Area rugs are great underfoot with a thick, beefy rug pad and are easily maintained since they can be moved. Not to mention they're a great, cost-efficient way to change up a room's decor when you get tired of them.

(See chapter 9, "Green Building," for more wood-flooring sources.)

Rapidly Renewable Flooring

Plant fibers such as bamboo, cork, and linoleum are fast-growing, renewable materials that make unique and environmentally sound statements when installed as flooring.

Bamboo grows quickly and is extremely hard. It takes four to seven years to regenerate, making it a better choice than oak or pine, which each take about twenty years. Bamboo comes in a very wide selection of colors and styles and is generally much less expense than FSC-certified hardwood. In one of our projects we installed hand-scooped bamboo that looked like an exotic hardwood; people are constantly surprised to learn it is really bamboo. Typically, bamboo is glued, not nailed down, so be sure to specify a nontoxic glue.

Cork is made from bark that has been peeled from Spanish oaks. Because it provides cushioning under feet and absorbs sound, kitchens and home spas are a great place to install this material. It is also a great insulator, hygienic, antiallergenic, water resistant, does not trap dirt or fungus, and is easy to maintain. I always had a hard time installing cork for flooring because I felt that it resembled a '70s family room. Although I loved the way cork can look on a wall, I was not a huge fan of cork on the floor.

Recently, we saw a house with cork mosaic on the floor of the wine cellar. People were bending down to touch it because no one knew what it was. Anytime people want to touch a material you've installed, it's a success. This particular product looks like ceramic penny tiles but is actually slices of used wine stoppers.

Once grouted and sealed, it's completely waterproof. It totally changed our minds about cork flooring.

Linoleum is made the same way it has been for decades, manufactured from linseed oil, sawdust, cork, and pigments all mixed together and backed by jute fiber. It is extremely resistant to fire and does not melt. Durable linoleum flooring can last for thirty to forty years. When its life cycle comes to an end, linoleum is biodegradable and can be composted.

Recycled rubber floors are an excellent choice if you are designing spaces for young children, basements, yoga studios, or a home gym. Tiles made from recycled rubber tires are safe, antimicrobial, waterproof, can be nontoxic, and have very good sound and temperature insulation. Rubber tiles come in many colors and textures and are extremely easy to install.

Hard Surface Flooring

Concrete, terrazzo, natural stone, and ceramic tile are the longest lasting of floor materials. Visit centuries-old ruins on the shores of the Mediterranean Sea and you'll experience gorgeous mosaic stone and cement floors that are still intact. You will be hard pressed to find flooring materials more durable than these. They also have beneficial health properties because they do not emit fibers, gases, or harmful by-products. They do not absorb smoke, fumes, or contaminants.

Refinishing a concrete floor is the best green choice of the hard surface flooring materials because the least amount of material must be applied. Old slabs can be given a gorgeous new life given the advances in grinding, hardening, coloring, and polishing technologies. New concrete floors are also a good choice if you specify a cement with fly ash content. Fly ash is a recycled by-product of power plants and reduces the amount of Portland cement (a labor-intensive material) that must be used. A new cement floor does not require a subfloor, so again, fewer materials and energy are needed.

Tile and terrazzo floors are easy to clean and can be made from pre and postconsumer recycled content.

The installers should be instructed to use low-toxic grouts, sealers, and glues. The bigger the tiles, the less grout you will need. Less grout means less possibility of mold buildup and, consequently, less cleaning.

Ceramic tile also has the benefit of being able to achieve the look of wood or natural stone without ever having to refinish or seal the tile. Additionally, individual damaged tiles can easily be replaced instead of entire sections of materials. Ceramic tile doesn't fade or discolor when exposed to UV rays. It can even withstand fire or floods.

Natural stone floors will last many lifetimes but may often require routine sealer applications as part of their maintenance. Choose eco-friendly sealers, glues, and grouts. If possible, specify a stone that is located in your region (within a five-hundred-mile radius). Most likely it will be less expensive and reduce the pollution that is created when a large amount of a heavy, foreign stone is delivered. Or specify from well-managed quarries.

Choosing the Right Tile for Every Room in Your Home

The materials you choose to install in your home are a big factor in both the aesthetic and function of the design of your home. Porcelain, glass, natural stone, marble, ceramic, all have different advantages and disadvantages that come into play based upon budget, location, and how they are used.

Choosing Tile for Bathrooms: Go for the Grip!

When choosing tile for your bathroom and shower floors, an aspect of tile you should take into consideration is its viscosity (how slippery or not the surface is). In areas like the bathroom (especially the shower) use an anti-slip tile or smaller application tile with more grout lines as a safety measure. The shower floor could use even smaller pieces of tile or mosaic where the grout will offer more grip.

In one of our aging-in-place/ADA/accessible-living projects, we used small mosaic tile on the entire bathroom floor that continued seamlessly into the shower without using a curb (which can be challenging for those who have a hard time lifting their foot or leg).

Photo by Stephen Busken.

broke the glass. We replaced the large glass with smaller bricks of glass and did the same for another project.

Choosing Tile for Outdoor Spaces

Something to consider in choosing outdoor tile is its UV resistance. If you're going for natural stone, a nonpolished finish would be a better choice to install around pool deck or a walkway with greater exposure to rain and other elements. Chlorine and salt can do damage to stone tile, so, in general, we recommend trying to avoid this type of tile. Instead of stone, opt for a porcelain tile.

Photo by Ken Hayden.

Choosing Tile for Kitchens: Backsplash and Walls

Backsplash and bathroom walls are a great opportunity to have fun and make a statement. This is your opportunity to have some fun and make a statement—go for color, 3D texture, rough stone, or antique glass.

But you'll still want to be careful about the placement: We had a project where we installed large slabs of antique mirror for a kitchen backsplash. Although the client was careful while cooking, their cleaning crew was not and had banged pots against the wall and

Glass and glazed porcelain make for awesome pool tile material. Glass is the most popular pool tile but also the most expensive. If you choose this type of tiling, be sure to select an iridescent color for the shimmering results. Mosaic tiles are another great idea, as they give the designers some creative flexibility when it comes to installing the tile.

And don't forget: when installing tile outdoors and around pools, chemical-resistant grout is a must! And to prevent powder staining, you will also want to make sure that your installer is using a grout release.

Photo by Stephen Busken.

Carpet

As a rule, our firm does not specify wall-to-wall carpeting. The reasons our firm takes a stance against wall-to-wall carpet is for the environment and human health. Most inexpensive carpets are made from nylon olefin, which is a toxic petrochemical derived from petroleum. These carpets contain formaldehyde, toluene, and xylene, which are all toxic to the nervous system.

They off-gas these fumes for many years—sometimes throughout their entire lifespan. When they are disposed of, most of them wind up in landfills and leach poisonous chemicals into the Earth. About 3.5 billion tons of used, toxic wall-to-wall carpeting and padding winds up in landfills every year. So, if you're going to use wall-to-wall carpeting, make sure to ask about the company's recycling program. The easiest to recycle is carpet made of natural fibers because it can be composted or used as a layer of mulch underneath wood bark or gravel to reduce weeds.

What about wool? Wool doesn't off-gas toxins, so it is a better environmental choice than synthetic carpet. But the problem, in addition to being cost prohibitive for most budgets, is that the backing of the carpet is loaded with highly reactive compounds and noxious glues. The padding is generally made of urethane and foamed with hydrocarbons such as methyl or bonded urethanes. These products contribute to sick building syndrome and all of the symptoms that come with it.

Avoid any carpet or pad that contains harmful chemicals, like stain protectors and other finishes. Check for Greenguard and Green Label certification.

Also problematic: Since wall-to-wall carpets are fixed to the floor, they can never really be cleaned thoroughly. You can vacuum multiple times, every day, with the best vacuums available, and you will never be able to get all of the dust, dirt, and microorganisms that are embedded in the three layers of carpet, backing, and padding.

This practically untreatable condition is the perfect environment for mold and fungus to grow, even without a lot of moisture in the room. The reality is that liquids are often spilled on carpets, and if they're not completely dry in a twenty-four-hour period, mold will most likely occur.

If you're involved in a remodel and have to remove wall-to-wall carpeting, cross your fingers—you could have a gorgeous wood, tile, or cement floor under the old carpet.

For people who just won't live without carpets, I suggest large area rugs made of natural or recyclable fibers. Natural carpet materials include wool, cotton, bamboo, jute, or hemp. When they are placed on hard surfaces, large rugs have the same benefits of softening an area, but they can also be removed for cleaning the rugs and the floor beneath them. Carpet tiles made of recycled and refurbished carpets are another option. If moisture, stains, or wear occur, you simply replace the individual carpet tile. These tiles do not emit fumes, which also makes them a greener choice.

We're big fans of carpets made from renewable materials. They tend to be inexpensive, look amazing, and add interesting texture to interior spaces. The Natural Carpet Company, in Los Angeles, has a superior selection of area rugs that meet all of these criteria.

WALLS AND CEILINGS

We love a great wall feature! Talk about elevating your space and drawing the eye up. The surfaces of walls and ceilings can be covered in paint, wallpaper, stone, tile, plaster, and paneling. The square footage of surface materials used on walls is more than any other surface in the home, creating potential health hazards if nontoxic products are not specified. Because walls are such a large part of any home, you have an extraordinary opportunity to make a design statement using a large portion of green materials that are healthy for the planet and the people occupying the space.

Paint

Primarily because paint is the least expensive product and has the least expensive application process for interior walls, a lot of it is used in residential homes. But when it comes to poor indoor air quality, paint is a major culprit. If you do not specify an eco-friendly paint, you are subjecting the occupants to volatile organic compounds (that "new paint" smell), carcinogens that can cause kidney damage, headaches, loss of muscle control, dizziness, and irregular heartbeats.

Many companies offer thousands of colors in formulas that contain no VOCs. However, "no VOC" doesn't mean the paint is entirely nontoxic. Most interior no- or low-VOC paints contain components that are derived from petroleum products. Check with the manufacturer that the paint you are using is water based. Water-based acrylics are less toxic, more affordable, and extremely durable. Green Seal or Greenguard can help you determine how green your paint is.

For people who are sensitive to the chemicals in low- or no-VOC paints, some manufacturers are producing natural paints, made from plant oils and minerals. We've come across a few manufacturers who claim their paint is so safe that you can eat it without getting sick (though we've yet to put that to the test ourselves).

Be sure to specify the appropriate sheen for each room. For instance, high-humidity rooms like kitchens and bathrooms need a high-sheen, durable paint because they are washed more frequently. Using lighter colors will help distribute daylight deeper into the home.

If you have leftover paint at the end of the project, don't dump wet paint into the trash or down a drain. If you must dispose of it, let it dry completely (latex paint is not hazardous once it has dried). Better, donate unused low- or no-VOC paint to a women's or children's shelter. If it's sealed properly, it will last a very long time. Many times, volunteers or the occupants will donate time to make improvements but lack the materials. Something as simple as the paint you no longer need can make all the difference!

Tile

Recycled tiles come in glass, ceramic, and porcelain made from recycled glass and preconsumer industrial waste. Unfortunately, the variety of size, color, and texture found in conventional tiles has not crossed over into the recycled product. The good news is that more and more vendors are adding recycled-content tiles to their lines. As with all green products, make sure the adhesives and backing are also nontoxic.

Plaster

Earth-based plasters are the healthiest wall finish. Natural clay plaster allows a wall to absorb and release moisture as needed. This amazing self-adjustment in the humidity levels of a room helps to ensure that the space is comfortable for its occupants and unlikely to develop mold.

It's undeniable that any well-installed plaster wall is irresistible to the touch, but earth plaster walls are actually good for your skin. The clay they use actually releases and absorbs moisture as it is needed in the

Photo by Ken Hayden.

Kitchen bar designed by Caine and Company, Scottsdale, AZ, featuring Lori Dennis, Inc. Flores Blanco Hex tile for bar. (Photo by Roehner + Ryan.)

Photo by Ken Hayden.

Photo by Ken Hayden.

interior. They're also made from natural pigments that have breathtaking hues. If your budget allows, this is one of the most scrumptious interior splurges you can buy. Plus, added moisture in the room where you sleep helps to hydrate skin (fewer wrinkles).

American Clay (www.americanclay.com) has been in the business of healthy walls for the past twenty-five years and has perfected it. Their line offers multiple finishes and a wide variety of colors. Any plaster professional can apply it, it's easy to repair when damaged, and the product looks simply elegant.

Wall Panels and Wall Coverings

Installing wall panels provides a dramatic way to dress a wall or separate areas in a room. When panels are installed directly on walls, they add to the thermal mass, which helps regulate heat and cold air exchange. Wall panel products can be made from eco-friendly materials and are an attractive and welcome change to paint and wall cover.

For many years, manufacturers offered PVC-based vinyl "wallpaper," which was cheap, extremely durable, and easy to clean. Eventually it became known that vinyl wall covering off-gases plasticizers (known endocrine disruptors) into your living space and into landfills when discarded. It is ironic that this is what lined nursing homes and hospital rooms for years. Light has been shed on the detrimental effects that PVC-based wall cover has on indoor air quality.

As a response, an entire green wall cover industry seemed to sprout overnight. Along with paint, environmentally friendly wall cover is one of the most plentiful, easy-to-find surface materials. These new products do not contain heavy metals or PVC. They are made from rapidly renewable sources like cork, grasses, and other plant fibers.

Even though most natural fibers are breathable, it is still best to avoid wall cover in humid areas, like bathrooms and home spas. If moisture condenses behind the wall covering, it can result in mold and rot.

Environmentally Friendly Wall Coverings

Finally, when the wall cover is applied, you must be certain that the green paper you specify is pasted with an equally environmentally friendly paste or glue. It completely defeats the purpose of purchasing a health-based wall cover when the adhesive behind it is off-gassing toxins into the room. The VOCs from the glue can literally get you high and not in a good way.

Dining room by Lori Dennis. Photo by Ken Hayden.

Wall panels from modularArts (www.modulararts.com) transform ordinary walls into extraordinary experiences. This home, owned by a DJ and a club promoter, sees its fair share of guests who expect to be wowed. The panels in the dining room are free of toxic chemicals, easy to install, and can be painted, but also look fabulous in their natural state, as shown in this photo.

Faux Stone

Unless you can specify a natural stone that is abundant and mined within five hundred miles of your project, a greener choice is faux stone. Using a faux stone product on the walls can save an enormous amount of labor, cost, energy, and natural resources. The advances in technology have resulted in a product that closely resembles nature.

In fact, Lori Dennis, Inc. won the *Southern Accents/ASID Best Green Design* award with a bedroom featuring a wall covered in faux stone. If it passed the approval of Southern style guru *Southern Accents* editor in chief Karen Carroll, you can feel confident about using it.

Bedroom by Lori Dennis. Photo by Christian Romero.

The bedroom features Eldorado stone, Anna Sova linens, a custom bed made of FSC-certified wood and AFM Safecoat stain, vintage lamps, and a painting by Tony Caputo. Clearly, the bedroom would not be the same without the dramatic use of stone. The twist is that this stone is generally applied to an exterior. With no reason to limit ourselves, we decided to bring the outdoors in.

Eldorado Stone (www.eldoradostone.com) has five manufacturing plants strategically located throughout the country, which means that 78 percent of the United States population lives within five hundred miles of an Eldorado plant. They recycle water in the manufacturing process and are committed to sourcing local, raw materials made with pre and postconsumer waste products. The product contributes thermal mass to the walls, helping insulate for heating and cooling and is half the weight of stone, resulting in reduced shipping pollution. The product is long lasting, with a fifty-year warranty. It also helps you to qualify for LEED points.

COUNTERS AND BACKSPLASHES

For our purposes, three things should be considered when installing counters and backsplashes. Is the material environmentally friendly, is it durable, and is it easy to clean? A green installation will consist of a product that meets all of these criteria. Many times, a homeowner is seduced by the words "natural stone" and incorrectly thinks those words represent a better product.

When we explain the toll "natural stone" has on the environment and the required upkeep, they become more willing to look at the green choice. The composite stone materials available today closely resemble stone, but do not require the maintenance of stone or the extraction and transportation consequences usually associated with natural stone. To convert the nonbelievers, we recently did a sample test of a gray limestone and engineered quartz. Everyone was shocked that they could not tell the difference.

Kitchen by Lori Dennis. Photo by Ken Hayden.

This is one of the most eco-friendly kitchens we've ever designed. The counters are Caesarstone, with cabinets by Valcucine. Gaggenau's greenest appliances were installed, and reclaimed oak panels adorn the walls. In addition to a serene palette that lets the food shine, our favorite part of the space is the floor-to-ceiling windows that allow natural light to dance throughout the kitchen.

Get Your Green Countertop On!

Tip #1: Skip the Granite. It's heavy and requires a lot of energy to mine it, shape it, and transport it to your project. Synthetic, recycled countertops utilize broken glass and porcelain, suspended in a resin, to create gorgeous, durable surfaces perfect for cooking, eating, and living. They are installed and work just like granite, but greener. A company like EnviroGLAS is a great one to shop for these alternatives.

Tip #2: Source Healthy Materials. Greenguard-certified products use recycled content and recycle industrial raw material. Seek out companies like Caesarstone that avoid using hazardous substances and whose countertops are impervious to mold and microbes.

Tip #3: Glassy and Maintainable. Brands like EnviroPLANK and EnviroSLAB terrazzo tiles and slabs are made of postconsumer and postindustrial recycled glass. The product is made from 75 percent recycled glass from local recycling programs for minimal transportation impact. The product is resistant to chips, stains, burns, and chemicals and has zero VOCs and virtually no emissions. Maintenance of the product requires only water, mild cleaner, and no wax. It is designed to last a lifetime but can be ground up for a new floor if desired.

SINKS AND TUBS

Using reclaimed or recycled sinks and tubs can accomplish green and aesthetic design goals. It keeps old products out of landfills, eliminates the need for raw materials or production of new products, and can make a charming interior style. Water conservation can be accomplished by installing screw-in aerators to control water flow (older toilets that flush with more than 1.6 gallons of water should not be installed). To prevent lead poisoning, make sure that any painted product made before 1970 is tested for lead.

There is a lot of scrap iron in the world. Most of it is just sitting in landfills, slowly oxidizing and rusting away. Kohler (www.kohler.com) has an entire line of tubs, sinks, fixtures, and accessories crafted from 97 percent recycled iron. They melt down products headed for the waste stream and make them into bubble tubs and sinks. It's possible the tub you sink into tonight was once a bumper for a '67 Ford Fairlane.

CABINETS

Many affordable conventional cabinets are made with pressed particleboard and veneers. Quite often the particleboard contains formaldehyde binders, which can off-gas for the life of the cabinets. To make matters worse, the clear finishes commonly applied to cabinets are made from urea-formaldehyde resins. This is probably not the healthiest place to store food, dishes, and utensils.

The exceptions to this rule are European cabinets, made of high-density fiberboard. Mandated by law in Europe, the chipboard that is used has to comply with a set standard of formaldehyde emissions. The European standard for chipboard is titled E1, confirming emission levels that are acceptable. In addition to the chipboard, European manufacturers use finishes and glue that comply with emission standards. Wheatboard covered in eco-friendly veneers is also a good solution to achieving affordably priced, environmentally sound cabinets.

When you have a bigger budget for solid wood cabinets, make sure the wood is FSC certified. The paints and finishing materials must also be no VOC and nontoxic.

The bar in this Hollywood Hills home features Treefrog eco-friendly veneer (one of our favorite surface materials) and Brookside FSC veneers. (Bar by Lori Dennis. Photo by Ken Hayden.)

Reusing existing cabinets is the greenest option of all. New doors and hardware can be added to existing boxes to achieve an entirely new look. If the cabinet configuration and door style still work but need updating, consider painting or refinishing. If you are removing cabinets, donate or relocate to a storage area to avoid having them end up in a landfill.

Finally, remember that a smooth cabinet surface is easier and quicker to clean.

It adds richness and dimension to interiors reminiscent of the work of '30s French masters like Ruhlmann and Jean-Michel Frank. Brookside and Treefrog are companies who carry exquisite and downright funky variations of the best that nature has to offer.

These companies exhibit environmentally responsible practices and harvest sustainable materials. The Treefrog veneered bar featured in this photo is an example of the magnificence you can achieve when you apply veneer to a surface. Caesarstone counters and a cellar of almost two hundred bottles of sommelier-selected wines leave you wanting even more.

HARDWARE

When it comes to shopping for hardware, seek out companies that are signatories to the United Nations Global Compact and are committed to updating their sustainability practices on an ongoing basis. Their products are made from nonhazardous materials and pass strict oversight when it comes to manufacturing in factories overseas. These companies are more likely to practice environmental responsibility by using green sand technology in the casting process. They participate in metal scrap- and office-recycling programs and provide healthy working conditions for their employees.

SEALERS, FINISHES, AND ADHESIVES

After spending the time and money to select green finishes, one of the big mistakes many people make is attaching or finishing them with toxic products. Natural products are a better alternative to conventional petroleum-based finishes. These healthier options have not yet been perfected, and you may sometimes have to sacrifice moisture resistance and an easy installation process for healthier air quality. That's a trade-off worth making! Here are a couple of our personal favorites:

Livos (www.livos.de/en/) offers low-VOC wood stains and finishes and technical data sheets on all of their products, which give relevant information of application ranges and product contents.

AFM Safecoat (www.afmsafecoat.com) has eliminated toxic ingredients such as solvents, heavy metals, chemical residues, and formaldehyde from their products. Paint, stain, and finish products literally contain a "safe coat" with a molecular formulation designed to seal surfaces, greatly reducing any off-gassing.

5

INTERIOR PLANTS

Most people know that plants can make a space look better but are unaware that they can also improve the air quality in a room and a person's health. According to the Environmental Protection Agency, most Americans spend 90 percent of their lives indoors, and interiors are five to ten times more polluted than the exterior. WHAT? When we first heard that, we didn't believe it—not in our houses, we're shoes-off neat freaks. But even an extremely clean house is filled with toxins from the plastic, computers, television, printer inks, dry-cleaned clothes, and on and on.

INTERIOR PLANTS AND INDOOR AIR QUALITY

One way to combat these symptoms is with indoor plants. They are known to clean the air, replenish it with oxygen helping reduce negative physical symptoms, and even make people more calm.

Rooms with plants have been measured as showing up to 60 percent fewer airborne molds and bacteria than rooms with no plants. They suck the toxins out of the environment and act as purifying organs, like the kidneys or lungs of the house.

Amazingly, the plants absorb the contaminants into their leaves and transfer them to their roots, where they digest them as food. They do this by releasing phytochemicals, acting as moisture, into the air in order to "catch" the dirty air around them, which they pull down into the roots. By releasing and absorbing humidity in the environment, plants are able to aid in regulating a comfortable climate.

Humans have also been known to become sick when humidity levels drop, so plants are essentially helping

us to ward off colds. English ivy is said to be one of the best plants to fight off colds. Small openings on the underside of a plant's leaves release moisture into the air, boosting humidity levels and helping to alleviate cold symptoms.

Because of English ivy's high volume of leaves, horticulturists recommend it as one of the most effective cold-fighting plants. On the flip side, too much moisture can be a bad thing if mold occurs. Mold becomes a problem when humidity levels become too high. Mold can wreak havoc on a structure and our bodies. Again, by helping regulate humidity, plants help control mold.

Research has shown that plants can improve our mood by increasing positive feelings. This improves creativity by producing higher dopamine levels, which control the flow of information to our brains. By also reducing noise pollution (neighbors, gardeners, car alarms), they allow us to concentrate and use our creativity. Because evolution has taught humans that plants are essential for survival, just seeing a plant can reduce stress levels by inducing a calming effect.

It has also been shown that during hot months, plants have a cooling effect. They are even said to produce a healthy drop in heart rate. Studies have shown people in rooms with plants had a four-point drop in their systolic heart rate after taking a stress test versus people taking the same test with no plants in the room. They had only a two-point drop.

Which plants are the best for clean interior air, and how many do you need? All plants will help clean the environment, but some will work harder than others at digesting the microbes that live in their potting soil and reversing the effects of the VOCs in your indoor environment. VOCs emitted from paint, furniture, carpets, and other carcinogenic off-gassers in your environment include formaldehyde, toluene, xylene, trichloroethylene, ammonia, carbon monoxide, and benzene. These are just a few of the toxins you live with and breathe in every day.

Formaldehyde is released by draperies, upholstery, paper towels, facial tissue, nail polish remover, grocery bags, plywood, particleboard, paints, stains, caulking, and varnishes. Xylene and toluene are released by human breath, computer screens, photocopiers, printers, stains, and varnishes. Benzene is released by tobacco smoke, printers, copiers, floor and wall coverings, particleboard, caulking, adhesives, paints, stains, and varnishes. Ammonia is released by cleaning agents, human breath, printers, and photocopiers.

NASA contracted an environmental engineer to perform a study on houseplants combating pollution. He exposed various plants to high levels of chemicals and found that the houseplants were able to remove 87 percent of air toxins in a twenty-four-hour period. Based on this study, NASA recommends fifteen to eighteen plants (in six- to eight-inch diameter pots) in a 1,800-square-foot home to purify indoor air.

The Best Plants for Indoor Air Quality, Human Health, and Well-Being

Gerber daisies are known to reduce formaldehyde and benzene.

Chrysanthemums help eliminate benzene, formaldehyde, ammonia, and trichloroethylene.

Orchids minimize xylene and toluene.

English ivy aids in the reduction of benzene levels and formaldehyde.

Bamboo combats formaldehyde levels.

Ficus is able to remove high concentrations of formaldehyde, benzene and trichloroethylene. Ficus is resistant to many household insects and will grow in full or semisun.

Dracaena (corn plant) removes formaldehyde.

Ferns remove formaldehyde and ammonia. They are easy to care for because they require little water, but they must be misted a few times a week, or the leaves will brown and drop. They thrive in indirect light. Ferns may be one of the oldest groups of plants, dating back to prehistoric times.

Palms (specifically areca and lady palm) reduce ammonia, formaldehyde, xylene, and toluene. The areca is consistently rated among the best household plants for removing toxins and should be kept in semishade. The lady palm is highly resistant to most plant insects, slow to grow, easy to maintain, and should also be kept in semishade.

Peace lilies can add up to 5 percent humidity to a room and reduce benzene, trichloroethylene, and acetone levels. Their best work is done in midlight to shade.

Spider plants remove benzene and formaldehyde.

Philodendrons can thrive without a lot of natural light, so they are ideal for darker areas of the interior where other plants cannot survive. Philodendrons are particularly effective in removing formaldehyde.

Janet Craig is a tropical shrub that grows eight to twelve feet tall. It has green leaves that are sometimes cultivated to a gray-green color. The plant has been shown by NASA to help remove formaldehyde, xylene, and toluene. One NASA study showed three Janet Craigs in a 130-square-foot room were able to cut 70 percent of the VOCs. This plant can tolerate dimly lit areas but does best in semishade.

If you are worried about killing your houseplants, snake plants are easy to maintain. Even in windowless rooms, they are effective at reducing indoor toxins.

Our personal favorites are succulents. They are extremely low maintenance and require little water. There are many varieties that bloom in brilliant colors. Since these plants are usually thought of as an exterior group, it is a delightful surprise to see them thriving indoors.

Jade plants, known as the "money tree," are particularly wonderful for interiors. They can be potted as

Photo by Roy Yerushalmi.

small table plants or allowed to grow into large trees. At certain times of the year, they bloom with clusters of small pink flowers, a truly perfect site.

The EPA and NASA are in agreement about the fact that indoor air quality is worse than outdoor. However, the EPA says that it would take hundreds of plants to duplicate the toxin-removing effects produced in the NASA studies. No matter who is right, it is a fact that plants add oxygen and humidity to the air, which has proven health benefits. All you have to do is look at plants and flowers, and you find yourself relaxing, sometimes even experiencing the corners of your mouth turning up; that has to be good for you.

CUT FLOWERS

Who doesn't love to get flowers? They're gorgeous, they smell good, and they make an interior look magazine ready. Cut flowers are an easy hostess gift and generally make anyone happy.

But there are some dirty secrets that no one ever tells you about cut flowers. About 80 percent of cut flowers are grown in South America, Africa, and Southeast Asia. Most of the time they are grown in greenhouses that use pesticides, herbicides, and fungicides that are banned in the United States. These include DDT and methyl bromide. The people who work in these greenhouses come into contact with these chemicals on a daily basis. Some of the symptoms they experience are skin and respiratory illness, birth defects, and impaired vision. If that isn't bad enough, the chemicals they are using are flushed into the earth and groundwater, causing serious problems for animal, bird, and fish populations. The pollution released into the groundwater also reduces levels of potable water.

These flowers are then sent thousands of miles, mostly to the United States, using millions of gallons of fuel and releasing large amounts of pollution into the environment on their journey. Once they reach the United States, they are sprayed with even more chemicals to kill any foreign insects. Even flowers grown in the United States, which don't have to travel as far and don't use banned chemicals, still use plenty of toxic pesticides and fertilizers that hurt our environment, people, and animals. (This could be occurring with plants as well, but plants are the lesser of two evils, as you can buy one plant that will last for many decades.)

For those of you who cannot bear to give up cut flowers, there is an easy alternative: buy local organic flowers. Most of the time, you can find seasonal varieties at your local farmers market, and they are usually pretty affordable.

If you have the space, try planting a cut flower garden of your own. Hydrangea is one of the most beautiful flowers, and the plant really grows like a weed (for most of the late spring until fall outside) in partial shade. In the living rooms chapter, we discuss outdoor gardens, so more on that subject soon. Of course, with any plant life you bring into your space, you want to be cognizant of the how the human and animal lives in your home interact with them. Be aware of allergies and plants that could be harmful to babies and pets, like lillies, poinsettias, and caladiums.

6

APPLIANCES AND PLUMBING FIXTURES

When selecting appliances and plumbing fixtures for a green home, pay close attention to water and energy conservation features in addition to performance. Energy Star's rating system has taken a lot of the guesswork out of selecting appliances that don't waste energy. The WaterSense label will lead you in the right direction for water-efficient fixtures. When you're buying new items, make sure to select quality materials that will last for decades. If you're purchasing salvaged materials, be certain that you are not sacrificing water or energy efficiency.

Designing in a water-wise manner will be required by law in the coming years. Studies say that in the next decade water shortages will be a serious worldwide problem. Our current water resources will not be sufficient anymore. If we want the next generation to have fresh water, we will need to take a new approach toward usage and waste.

CONSERVATION IS KEY

There are too many people on this planet to waste fresh water. The water that comes from the tap is not limitless. Water is a finite resource, and it is getting expensive.

As we continue to pollute it with manufacturing, waste, and toxic chemicals, clean water becomes scarce. The human population is growing faster than our freshwater supply and will not continue to meet our needs in the next century if we do not change our ways. We often wonder why, with a planet that is made up of three-quarters water, albeit saltwater, we haven't come up with a better solution for desalinization. But that's a discussion for another day and still not an excuse to waste water.

Wasting energy by using nonrenewable resources negatively effects the environment by depleting valuable resources that cannot be replaced, creating air pollution and emitting greenhouse gases. Most of the energy used to power American households comes from sources such as coal- and oil-fed power plants. The carbon emissions from these plants wreak havoc in our atmosphere and are said to cause human illness and speed up climate change. Specifying appliances that use energy in the most efficient manner helps to slow down carbon emissions.

WHAT MAKES THIS HOME GREEN?

Energy-efficient everything? Check! It's the architectural features like the brick stone walls, Caesarstone kitchen counters, lighting, and flooring that define the character of this modern farmhouse loft in Los Angeles. The RomaBrick from Eldorado

Photo by Erika Bierman.

FARMHOUSE LOFT

Photos by Erika Bierman

Eldorado Stone helps homeowners and trade professionals select products that embody the rich color, texture, and character of the landscapes surrounding them, which makes them perfect inspiration for any green interior design, not to mention they are affiliated with the US Green Building Council.

In the library, we used three Four Hands freestanding bookshelves and bunched them together to create a wall with a "built-in" look. We created custom cocktail tables in cluster configurations in the living room, made from FSC woods. And we reused and repurposed the client's existing accent furniture wherever possible!

Layered lighting was essential in this home: all lighting is LED and dimmable. Pro designer tip: Install large-scale mirrors opposite windows whenever possible to bounce natural light around, like we did here in the farmhouse living room. Maybe you'll end up using less electricity? (Maybe a stretch, but we like to push green to its extremes whenever possible!

You'll find Jaipur rugs throughout the space and organic linens used on everything from the dining chair slipcovers to the organic cotton bedding.

Stone runs throughout the wall features in this Los Angeles modern farmhouse, proving the perfect backdrop for neutral furnishings and lighting to pop against. It gives the space its organic, unique texture.

GET THE LOOK: MODERN FARMHOUSE STYLE IN FIVE SIMPLE STEPS

First: What is the modern farmhouse look? Marked by its tactful combination of rustic pieces and sleek accents, the modern farmhouse look is an incredibly warm, welcoming aesthetic. It is an indicator of tailored, designer taste, but it is also lived in. It's not stuffy or off-putting, as overly embellished or overly edited rooms can sometimes be. The modern

farmhouse has increased in popularity due to the demand for the "Restoration Hardware" look. But actually achieving the style is as much about the architectural details of the home as it is about the furnishings, accessories, and textiles.

1. **Attractive Opposites.** The modern farmhouse style marries a number of design opposites together: new and old, black and white, heavy and light. The style's popularity is due in part to its appeal to both traditionalists' and minimalists' aesthetics, because unlike many other interior styles, the modern farmhouse doesn't have to be one or the other necessarily.

Water-saving plumbing fixtures were installed throughout the home.

2. **Personalizing.** The modern farmhouse is an open look, both literally and metaphorically speaking: there is an emphasis on great rooms, high ceilings, wide-open plains. Within that space there is room for multiple styles to play. There are many subgenres of the modern farmhouse, if you will: some spaces allow more of the modern, industrial elements to take center stage, some evoke a more chintz-centric Americana feel, and others are reminiscent of a tasting room at a Sonoma vineyard. Play pretend for a minute: What kind of "farm" is this house on?

3. **Clean Lines for a Contemporary Flair.** Often, the rustic elements shine through in the architecture of the space and in streamlined furnishings: reclaimed wood, exposed beams and brick, barn doors, sectional sofas, metal bed frames, shiplap. The modern farmhouse aesthetic is one that is respectful of architecture: the furnishings directly complement *or* deliberately call attention to how they contrast with the structure they are in.

4. **Neutral Color Palettes.** There are, of course, exceptions to this rule, but oftentimes mastering the modern farmhouse is best with an earthy palette: natural woods, beiges, grays, and high-contrast black and white. On the occasion that a modern farmhouse includes pops of color, they're generally blues and greens or yellows that fit comfortably within the naturalistic palette. You're also more likely to find color used in a farmhouse-styled space that is closer to the beach. You probably won't find much neon or many jewel tones in these spaces!

5. **Family-Centric Spaces.** The modern farmhouse is all about celebrating family. Spaces are laid out for optimal entertaining: porches and patios have ample, comfy seating; great rooms flow seamlessly into spacious kitchens with deep farmhouse sinks. Combining industrial and rustic elements with a traditionally homespun aesthetic makes the modern farmhouse a truly timeless style. It's a patchwork quilt of design aesthetics, accommodating the busy schedules of everyone who inhabits the home.

WATER AND ENERGY USAGE

The following websites compare water and energy usage:

- **Energy Star** (www.energystar.gov/products) lists all of the Energy Star products available on the market. The site gives information on how much energy and water are saved per manufacturer or model number.
- **The American Council for an Energy Efficient Economy** (www.aceee.org) gives energy ratings of appliances.
- **Green-e** (www.green-e.org) provides customers clear information about green electricity products to help them make informed purchases and encourages the use of products that minimize air pollution and reduce greenhouse gas emissions.
- **Consumer Reports' Greener Choices** (www.consumerreports.org/food-labels/seals-and-claims) informs consumers about environmentally friendly products and offers reliable, practical sources of information on how to buy green and avoid "greenwashed" products.

TOILETS

Toilet flushing is the single largest use of water in most homes. In 1992, federal law mandated that new residential toilets use no more than 1.6 gallons per flush. Understandably, consumers were concerned about the ability of these "new" toilets to get the job done properly. The EPA has responded by allowing the WaterSense program to give approval to models that have passed a performance test.

We now realize that 1.6 gallons per flush is an incredible amount of fresh water to flush down a drain, and as a result, plenty of alternative toilet technology is now widely available. Dual-flush toilets (lower volume flush for liquid, stronger volume for solids), common in European countries, are starting to become more prevalent in America. They use approximately 20 percent less than the 1.6-gallon amount required by law.

And sometimes the most obvious solutions are best. Make sure you specify a wastebasket in every bathroom. This helps to prevent the toilet from being used as a wastebasket.

Dual-Flush Toilets

Dual-flush toilets have two buttons, one for solid and one for liquid. Since a liquid requires less force to flush, the corresponding button allows the toilet to use less water.

Kohler (www.us.kohler.com) is a leader in dual-flush technology. They have gone thorough exhaustive testing to ensure that each toilet is as quiet as possible and has great flushing capability.

TOTO (www.totousa.com) practices sustainable manufacturing, engages in life-cycle assessment for their products, and even has a toilet that eliminates the need for paper.

Composting Toilets

Composting toilets have been around since the 1930s in Scandinavian countries. They require no water, are cost effective, and require less maintenance than conventional septic tank or sewer line toilet systems.

Envirolet sells attractive, low-profile, odorless systems that use organic products for waste elimination. They come in a variety of colors, including a girly, hot pink. And we never thought I'd be able to use the word "girly" to describe a composting toilet.

Bio-Sun Systems (www.best-composting-toilet.com) toilets use no chemicals and are odorless due to their forced ventilation system that accelerates waste breakdown, so there is not much to clean out except mild compost every two to five years.

Gray-water Toilets

Until recently, gray water in America had been considered waste, even though it is a perfectly good source for flushing toilets and irrigating landscapes. Using gray water has many benefits, including reducing consumption of water, lessening the loads on municipal water systems and treatment plants, reducing energy usage, and allowing the water tables to recharge.

The Water Toilet System by Alison Norcott (www.yankodesign.com) is an intelligent design in which the wastewater from the shower is stored in an in-wall tank and then used to flush the toilet. To avoid bacteria growth, the tank is discharged on a cyclic basis so that water isn't stored for over twenty-four hours. The toilet looks and functions like a gorgeous, conventional wall-mounted unit.

Caroma's (www.caromausa.com) Profile Smart 305 won the *Popular Mechanics* Breakthrough award for 2008, and I can see why. With an attached sink that fills the tank for the next flush when you wash your hands, this space saving toilet has a dual-flush feature and is easily installed.

FAUCETS AND SHOWERHEADS

Low-flow faucets and showerheads can save a home tens of thousands of gallons of water every year. New technology in faucet aerators reduces water flow by 60 percent and typically saves three gallons of water every minute. In the bathroom, encourage

Photo by Ron Gallemore.

homeowners to take shorter showers with faucets that have temporary turnoff valves for lathering body and hair. Custom shower systems with multiple showerheads or rain panel components will probably increase water consumption. If you're going to specify these types of systems, balance out the water use by installing a gray-water system for irrigating the landscape.

In order to use fewer cleaning products, specify matte plumbing fixtures instead of chrome or other shiny surfaces. The matte surface won't show as many water spots.

Installing drains in showers and tubs with baskets to catch hair can prevent clogs, which will eliminate the need to flush drains with harsh chemicals.

WASHERS AND DRYERS

The efficiency of the washing machine has improved dramatically over the last few years. Europeans have been using front-loading machines for years, but now they are common in American homes. They use about half the water of a top-loading model because the interior does not need to be filled with water to ensure all of the fabrics will get wet. Sixteen thousand gallons of water per household per year can be saved per household by using front-loading washing machines.

They are gentler on your clothing and use less energy to operate. The front-loading machines also spin much faster than top loaders, so more moisture is extracted from clothing, which reduces drying time. One note of caution: Make sure you are ready to go once you close the door and the water begins to fill the machine. The door will not open until the cycle is over because the water will spill everywhere.

When laundry machines are installed over finished spaces, make sure there is a water collection pan to prevent water damage in the event of a burst or leaking hose.

Line dry when time and space permit—this is done in most countries. When a dryer is used, be sure that

you have specified a model with a moisture sensor. The heat turns off when the fabrics are dry, saving energy and extending the life of the fabric.

The wave of energy-efficient steam washers and dryers is a breakthrough in water and energy conservation. Washers use less water than front-loading models, they run for less time, and the clothes don't end the cycle as wet, so they take even less time to dry. Not only do clothes come out cleaner and more sanitized, they are also odor-free and less wrinkly in the steam dryer.

Both Energy Star—rated Whirlpool and GE are leaders in the steam washer/dryer game.

WATER FILTERS

Installing water filters for drinking and bathing water eliminates chlorine and pesticides from the home's water supply, making the water safer and tastier. Kitchen filtration systems encourage homeowners to drink water from the tap, reducing the number of plastic bottles that will need to be recycled or end up in landfills. Filtration systems can treat water by reverse osmosis, ultraviolet, and the well-known, least expensive, highly effective carbon filtering. Carbon filters should be replaced after three to six months of regular usage.

DISHWASHERS

A fully loaded dishwasher will commonly use less water than hand-washing dishes, which means dishwashers are inherently the better choice for water conservation. Couple this with selecting models that use the least amount of water. All newer models use heat to wash the dishes, so select machines with booster heaters. If the homeowner is using a conventional water heater, this will allow them to set it at a lower temperature and still get the dishes sparkling clean. Maintaining the machine by clearing the food scrap basket will help the machine to operate at its highest efficiency.

Miele dishwashers are a kitchen's best friend and our firm's appliance of choice. Quiet, efficient, and superbly designed machines conserve water while getting the job done right for grimy dishes or dainty crystal.

DISPOSALS

The greenest kitchens won't have disposals. Instead, all food waste will be recycled in a compost pail and used as fertilizer for soil. Less water will be wasted, and less garbage will have to be processed. People who practice this type of recycling tend to have less waste because they are more aware of the amount of waste they are creating. If composting is not for you, it's still better to skip the disposal and throw the food in the trash. Food sent down the drain negatively affects aquatic life and wastes electricity and about

two thousand gallons of water per year. Food waste in the trash, or the yard waste receptacle, will eventually decompose.

REFRIGERATORS

Meet or exceed Energy Star standards when you select a refrigerator. Ice or water in the door will lower your energy performance. Top-mount freezers are the most efficient and side-by-side models are the least when comparing the same size refrigerators. Don't buy a larger refrigerator than is necessary. Properly clean and maintain the refrigerator to ensure optimal performance; this includes periodically vacuuming the coils.

Photo by Ron Gallemore.

OVENS AND STOVES

In most kitchen remodels, even ones in which people don't do much cooking, a routine request is that we select a commercial-quality range. Unless someone really cooks and knows how or is willing to learn to use a commercial range, we try to talk them out of it. If you are going to specify commercial ranges, you must also specify pots and pans that will work with them. Be careful not to purchase aluminum cookware, as aluminum has been linked to Alzheimer's disease. Teflon-coated cookware is also a problem because it contains perfluorochemicals, which are carcinogenic. Clay, stainless steel, ceramic, glass, porcelain, and cast-iron cookware are better choices.

Ovens and ranges do not have Energy Star ratings yet, but there are eco-friendly types of cooking appliance companies. Induction cooking uses much less energy than convection cooktops because all the heat goes directly to the pot instead of escaping into the room. Induction cooktops allow you to boil water in a matter of minutes, so you save time and energy. The minute you remove the pot, the heat source is cool, which is good news if you accidentally touch a burner. Jennair, Bosch, Wolf, and Viking offer induction cooktops. GE has a free-standing model with a convection oven on the bottom.

When specifying outdoor barbeques, chose electric, propane, or natural gas instead of charcoal or wood briquettes.

HOODS

Using ventilation hoods while cooking helps to eliminate indoor air pollution caused by smoke and food particles. Selecting an Energy Star–rated model will help ensure that there is less noise and energy usage generated. They also feature high-performance motors and improved blade design, which provides better performance and lengthens the life of the appliance.

MICROWAVES

The reviews are mixed on microwaves. Some environmentalists say they are better than conventional cooking methods because they heat food so quickly. Other scientists say that microwaves break down the natural structure of food, making it less nutritious. When plastics and high-fat foods are cooked in the microwave, dioxin is released into the food and, ultimately, into our bodies. Maybe that's reason enough to go microwave free?

Another reason to go microwave-free is for weight control. When you have to pull out a pot and reheat something, it takes time and effort. You really have to be hungry to go through that routine! If you're going to install a microwave, select a new model. All newer microwave heating is more efficient.

VACUUMS

Vacuuming once daily is one of the easiest and most effective ways to improve indoor air quality and prevent allergies. You would be amazed at the amount of dust that accumulates on a floor in a twenty-four-hour period. In addition to human and pet skin and hair, fine particles from rugs, furniture, window treatments, and other surfaces end up in the air and eventually on the floors as the items break down over time.

DEHUMIDIFIERS

Dehumidifiers absorb excess moisture in the air, which can cause mold and mildew. Chose an Energy Star–rated model that has enough capacity to run in the desired space. Most dehumidifiers have an automatic shut-off valve to prevent overflowing when the water tray becomes full; make sure yours does too. This helps to avoid accidental flooding.

Some models have hoses that drain the water into a specified area. This eliminates having to carry heavy buckets of water through the interior. Also important is the selection of a model that has a built-in humidistat, a device which allows you set the desired temperature for the room or home. The machine turns off when this temperature is reached. If the entire home needs to be dehumidified, there are whole-home models.

SMART HOME SYSTEMS

Smart home automation systems allow you to control music, movies, lights, temperature, landscape irrigation, and security systems from anywhere in your home or the world. By organizing the systems of the home to work together, you not only gain control over these systems but also conserve energy. Room temperatures are regulated with in-home keypads or remotely, and the systems even automate shades to open and close with the sunlight, reducing the work the climate control system has to do. Indoor and exterior lighting are controlled with programmable timers, dimmers, and motion sensors for the highest efficiency. Audiovisual media use power-sensing wireless outlet switches, which eliminate the need for power-hungry standby modes by cutting power to A/V devices when they are not in use. Even security systems can be integrated with the rest of the home.

With all the pros surrounding home automation, there is a con to consider. Products like Amazon's Alexa have recorded entire private conversations and sent them to people in the user's contact list. Whoopsie! If you want to ensure conversations remain private, be careful about saying things that your devices can hear. You may not have anything to hide, but it could be pretty embarrassing if your mother-in-law or boss hears what you really think of them.

7

LIVING ROOMS

After reading chapters 2 through 6, you have the essential ingredients to make your design project green. The next step is to combine these pieces in a sustainable manner. Your success in accomplishing an environmentally friendly space will be the result of careful thinking about how to assemble these materials and furnishings and how space is used. The design of an eco-friendly home relies heavily on the concepts of creatively using all of its living spaces, including the outdoors, and doing more with less. It requires a completely different approach toward possessions and dwellings that places more value on quality than quantity.

Pay close attention to the way European city dwellers live. Everything is compact; they have fewer things, yet they live very elegant, well-appointed lives. Conversely, many North Americans have rooms that are rarely used, yards that are frequently deserted, and a lot of things they don't need or use, but continue to store, wasting valuable space and energy to maintain. By building smaller dwellings with cleverly utilized spaces, filling them with possessions that are truly important to a lifestyle, and taking advantage of outdoor areas, whether a private yard or a public park, you can truly maximize your "living rooms" while simultaneously saving resources, energy, and pollution.

BUILDING SMALL

One of the most common questions we hear pertaining to a green project is, "How much will it cost me to go green?" Knowing what we know, it's easy to reply with, "How much will it cost you if you don't go green?"

This book has illustrated, chapter after chapter, how wasteful behavior costs us more than money. It threatens our health and future generations' existence on our magnificent planet. That's why we look at economic downturns as an opportunity to revisit the lessons of conservation taught to us by our parents and grandparents.

This responsible way of thinking has resulted in an interest in smaller, healthier, well-built, energy-efficient homes. In the past few years we've seen more than one headline discussing the death of the McMansion. Thankfully, we are now seeing the principles of sustainability becoming mainstream and an increase in behavior that values sensibility over excess. Showing off how much we have is simply out of style.

The fact is that the average family size has been declining for thirty-five years. We just don't need such big homes anymore. Finally, we are starting to see a shift in our culture of returning to what makes sense. According to *USA Today*, new homes, after doubling in size since 1960, are shrinking for the first time in decades. The average square footage of single-family homes has fallen from 2,629 to 2,343. With the focus on less square footage, an emphasis on good design with regard for our future becomes imperative.

Build as small as you can, because smaller homes are simply more efficient. They use less energy and raw materials to build and produce considerably less construction site waste. Once they're up and running, they take less energy to clean, heat, cool, and furnish. Additionally, less square footage amounts to lower labor and material costs. So an added bonus of building smaller is that you have a larger percentage of the budget to spend on quality materials that add value to the home and your portfolio.

The Atlantic chair from Cisco is the perfect small-scale design, made to relax. It has a swivel and a glider; you can rock yourself to sleep. The 100 percent Belgian linen slipcover is easy to remove to clean. For purchasing locations, visit www.ciscohome.net. (Photo by Dunja Dumanski.)

Building small also inspires innovative solutions to design problems, resulting in more unique and interesting living spaces. Even retailers are paying attention to the trend of smaller homes. Stores like Crate & Barrel, Cisco Brothers, and West Elm carry smaller-scaled lines of furniture, and appliance manufacturer Fagor is selling more of its combo washer/dryer units than ever before.

An additional benefit to smaller homes is a feeling of connectedness to a community. People with less private interior spaces tend to take advantage of what the community has to offer. Libraries, parks, swimming pools, civic centers, coffee shops, and museums offer opportunities to come into contact with your neighbors.

ELIMINATING "STUFF"

The easiest way to gain square footage for living space is to get rid of things you don't need or use. Good organization of important, necessary items is the key to being able to live in smaller spaces. The main reason we think we need so much space is because we have too much stuff.

If you have items that you aren't using, give them away, donate them to a charity, or sell them. Don't allow them to become old, damaged, and eventually useless. When you get something new, get rid of the old thing it replaced. This is especially useful with clothing. If you haven't worn an item in a year, you probably never will again. Pass it on to someone who will!

Unless you truly love something for its aesthetic value or it really serves a purpose, seriously consider getting rid of it. Not only will you gain space, but you will also have less to clean and maintain. So you gain time and money by saying bye-bye to clutter.

OPEN FLOOR PLANS

We've been building homes the same way for the last one hundred years by separating spaces for individual uses. The fact that this isn't working for modern life is validated by the popularity of the great room and live-work loft spaces. In shelter magazines, for sale listings, on home improvement shows—everywhere we look, live-work loft spaces are front and center. Ironically, these wide-open, multipurpose spaces actually bring us full circle to the times when all living was done in one space. Think igloos, teepees, and cabins with potbelly stoves.

Half the battle is already won—because people are embracing these new configurations of space, you won't need to convince them to forgo their walls. However, it requires a shift in traditional space-planning skills, especially when you are limited in square footage. It becomes essential to lose the idea of individual spaces for kitchen, dining, living room, and the den. Instead, design a "great space" that meets the needs of all of the public living areas.

The popular loft style embodies these very principles. In these configurations, single, well-thought-out rooms keep occupants connected while allowing them to perform individual tasks. But because so many activities are occurring in one space, it is crucial to install furniture and durable materials that are easy to clean and contain plenty of clever storage options.

Doing most of your living in one main area does fit a lot of life into less square footage, but there are also issues of privacy and noise that must be addressed.

Photo by Roy Yerushalm.

Fit life into less
square footage.

One of the most successful ways to create quiet, private spaces is to incorporate sliding doors, which act as temporary room dividers, into your plans. Simply open or close them to accommodate different activities. Plants, rugs, and fabric on furniture or window treatments also help absorb sound.

We removed a wall separating the kitchen from the living room to create an open plan in this home. The open space accommodates a variety of activities allowing cooking, entertaining, and lounging to occur simultaneously. There's plenty of space in the room for people to spread out and feel like they aren't on top of each other.

MULTIPURPOSE SPACES

Whether or not you chose an open floor plan, designing green challenges you to work on plans where spaces have multiple functions. Instead of immediately turning to the solution of adding square footage when more space is required, brainstorm how you can repurpose rooms that are rarely used, like formal living rooms and dining rooms. Maybe they'd be better suited as a home gym, home theater, home office, or wellness retreat?

Some of the most charming dining rooms we've seen double as libraries, which inspired us to use this technique in many Lori Dennis, Inc. projects. Most formal dining rooms, used only a few times a year, are a wonderful place to do things like plan menus, do homework, work on projects, and research.

Think outside the box. A dining room with extra-deep banquettes can be used for additional sleeping quarters in its off-hours, creating an instant guest room in smaller homes. Something as simple as placing a sofa on at least one side of the table makes the room feel like you're in a boutique hotel lounge and provides a perfect spot to curl up with a book when other areas of the home are occupied with noisier activities. This furniture arrangement works well in any style interior.

Installing a soft banquette next to a dining table serves two purposes. First, it allows the maximum

Photo by Mark Tanner.

number of diners to enjoy meals in this relatively small space. Second, it easily transforms into a comfortable area for afternoon naps or overnight guests.

This long and narrow dining room is the result of removing an outdated and never-used wet bar area and transforming it into a truly usable space. A backless bench is pushed against one wall and a sofa the client already owned is placed against the other wall. Entry is available from either side of the room. An oversized floor mirror rests against the far wall to reflect the good times and make the room seem more spacious. The light-filled space is also a cozy area for curling up with a book.

Rarely used formal living rooms are another great way to recapture space. Instead of waiting to enter this area only when special guests arrive, consider using it as a small home office or a multimedia or music room. The growing trend in home offices has resulted

Dining room by Lori Dennis. Photo by Ken Hayden.

in manufacturers designing attractive furniture with plenty of storage space that blends in with other living spaces. Installing a pretty secretary that secretly houses a computer and printer creates an instant home office that can be hidden when the room is used for other purposes. A beautiful desk and bookshelves can be incorporated into any space, even the most formal of designs. The seating already present in living room design accommodates any guests that may visit "the office." We don't know about you, but we much prefer to work in rooms filled with natural light and sensational furnishings as opposed to a commercial-looking office.

Formal living rooms also double nicely as music rooms. Whether it was coming from musical instruments, radios, or recordings, listening to music in the living room was a popular activity before television arrived. It's still a civilized way to use space. Lori installed a disco ball on her ceiling, and the living room doubles as a Friday-night karaoke/dance party space.

Create attractive displays for instruments and hidden storage for less attractive items like music books, gaming consoles, and LPs. Even if you don't actually play an instrument, video games like *Rock Band*, *Guitar Hero*, and karaoke machines allow anyone to enjoy the sensation. Using the living room as a place to enjoy music adds life to the space and allows the space to live up to its name.

Consider using a hallway as a mini gallery or for coat or purse storage. Displaying a collection of sculptures, paintings, or photographs in the same manner as a museum makes traveling through any hall an entertaining experience. Placing hooks along a hall for coats and purses helps to alleviate the need for more closet storage and reminds you of all the stylish choices that might have been forgotten had they been stashed in a closet.

While you may recognize the value of designing for and living in less space, you're probably wondering how you are going to fit the furniture necessary for so many functions into a smaller space. You do it by designing multitasking furniture pieces. For example, a dining table that lives behind the sofa can serve three purposes: a wider version of a console table with lighting, a desk during the day, and a dining table at night. You can pull it away from the back of the sofa and even add leaves when you need to accommodate more people.

Tables with shelves under them can be good hidden storage by placing a floor-length tablecloth on them. This is also a great way to change up a look. We love using a long, low (twenty-inch) bookshelf with cushions for seating on the ends and a television stand in the middle. Put baskets on the shelves containing packing supplies, throws, books, and baby toys. You'll have extra seating when entertaining a full house along with plenty of storage.

A final consideration in multipurpose spaces is that the lighting needs to be adaptable for each use. Even the most well-designed room will go flat without proper lighting. For example, a dining room that also serves as a library will require varied amounts of lights, as will a living room that doubles as an office or music room. Of course, it's always best to have as much natural light as possible throughout the day.

For night, plan on a variety of lighting fixtures, including recessed lighting, cove lighting, sconces, and table and floor lamps. They should all be on energy-efficient dimmers to accommodate the individual "moods" desired in these spaces.

REORGANIZING FOR REUSE

Before you buy anything, try to reuse what you own. It's one of the most basic and least expensive ways to go green. Doing this has no environmental impact and saves you money for other parts of the project. It almost sounds like it's too easy of a solution, but it really works. We call it "shopping at home."

Begin by moving things around. During our photo shoots, it is routine to move items in the room to new places to accommodate the camera's view. We always find that at least one of the changes turns out to be for the better and leave the new arrangement intact after the camera is long gone.

One of our favorite "shop at home" success stories was during the photoshoot of a sprawling, Mediterranean-style home in the Coachella Valley. By the time the client finished building the home, he had spent seven million dollars and completely exhausted his budget. There was nothing left for new furniture.

Begrudgingly he installed his old furniture. The rooms felt overcrowded and dated, with matching sets of bulky furniture throughout the home. It wasn't a big surprise when he wasn't happy with the results. However, where he saw a problem, we saw an opportunity to rearrange what he had and make it feel new.

The two key areas that were the most problematic were the living room, missing a sofa, and the entry hall, which felt empty without any furniture. The client planned to wait to purchase a new sofa and a round, wooden table in the entry. But we had other plans.

Photos by Ken Hayden.

Scouting the home looking for solutions, we found that his master bedroom was overcrowded in the sitting area. Removing the sofa from the bedroom accomplished two design goals: a more contemporary, spacious look in the bedroom, and we had our "new" living room sofa. We added a few throw pillows and a new rug, and the design fell into place.

We found a console table that was crowding a hallway and repositioned it in our entry. It worked even better than the round table we had envisioned for the space. The photographer was amazed; the

Entry by Lori Dennis. Photos by Ken Hayden.

client couldn't stop thanking us. The client's home was "newly" furnished without spending a dime or using any new resources. If this type of "working it out" will suffice in the high-end of traditional, it will certainly work in more flexible and forgiving styles, too. Finding creative solutions is far more rewarding and environmentally responsible than spending money and buying unnecessary things.

HOW SPACE IS USED

Really think about how the space will be used. Is it a place for entertaining, relaxing, gardening, sports, pets, a playground for children, or all of the above? Is there insufficient space inside? Will the outdoors relieve interior space concerns?

What are the views you want to see from the interior? From the exterior? How will the indoor and outdoor spaces relate to each other? How can you utilize the outdoors in most types of weather? Does the space need to be protected from the sun, pollution, or noise? How can you include landscaping that drains properly and minimizes outdoor water consumption or harmful maintenance chemicals?

You must also take into consideration what is already there and how to preserve natural conditions. Ask yourself the following questions. How do you protect existing trees, vegetation, and natural habitats? How will the current interior lighting affect the exterior moods? How do you maintain soil retention? Are there current natural or man-made structures that can be incorporated into the design?

Only when you have answers to these types of questions should you begin making an exterior plan.

KILL YOUR LAWN

Frequently, large areas of grass—lawns—are default solutions to exterior space planning. When you really think about the concept of maintaining a conventional lawn, it begins to make less and less sense to have one.

Traditional lawns require an enormous amount of maintenance, which creates various environmental burdens. In order for a lawn to be lush and green, it typically requires regular applications of fertilizers and pesticides. When the rain comes, these chemicals run off into sewers, which require treatment or, worse, pollute waterways.

In many parts of North America, lawns need to be artificially irrigated, which places unnecessary strains on freshwater supplies.

The thing we find most absurd about lawns in the constant desire to make them grow only to have to cut and trim them weekly. Don't we have enough responsibilities in our lives? Adding to the offenses, gas-operated mowers, trimmers, and weed whackers emit noxious fumes and pollution. Replacing a lawn with indigenous plants, edible gardens, permeable paving, or wildlife habitats will create a significant decline in the amount of toxic runoff, wasted energy, and pollution. It will also save a homeowner money and a tremendous number of man-hours in the long run.

If there is already a significant lawn in place, there will be considerable costs to remove and replace it with another solution. This cost is typically lower, however, in comparison to the cost of maintaining a lawn.

If you just can't do without the lawn, try to install only the minimum amount needed for dogs or children. Plant native turfgrasses or wild grasses, which are more drought tolerant, potentially fire resistant,

Photo by Roy Yerushalm.

Photo by Roy Yerushalm.

and require fewer fertilizers and pesticides and less maintenance.

Artificial turf is also an option. Companies like SYNLawn (www.synlawn.com) and EasyTurf (www.easyturf.com) supply realistic-looking synthetic grass that requires little maintenance and no water or chemicals.

NATIVE PLANTS AND WILDLIFE

Planting indigenous, regional plants requires a lot less environmental burden. These types of plants tend to need little, if any, chemical pesticides or herbicides because they have adapted to their climate and soil conditions. The occasional addition of compost and beneficial insects is about the only booster shot needed for native plants to flourish.

When planting, consider species that contain berries, flowers (nectar), and seeds, as they will encourage wildlife like butterflies, honeybees, and hummingbirds to visit the garden. Unless you have visited such a place, you cannot imagine the peaceful feeling you get from seeing these little creatures buzz around.

Native flower varieties can also be planted in cutting gardens as a simple, convenient alternative to buying chemical-laden, store-bought flowers. Pollinated and fragrant species will penetrate indoor living areas, so be sure to ask the homeowner about any plant allergies.

EDIBLE GARDENS

Although we tend to think of a residential yard as a private space, the yard can really be an opportunity

Photo by Mark Tanner.

their own produce may be a bit less liberal with the toxic chemicals on it.

When you plant certain varieties of herbs and flowers together, they give the added benefits of improving soil, preventing harmful insect infestation, and increasing propagation in your garden.

- Mint planted with tomatoes and cabbage deters ants, fleas, cabbage moths, rodents, and aphids and attracts earthworms.
- Planting garlic near cucumbers, celery, peas, lettuce, raspberries, and roses wards off Japanese beetles and spider mites, and keeps aphids off roses.
- The combination of lavender, roses, and fruit trees keeps moths away but attracts beneficial bees, ladybugs, and praying mantises.
- Borage planted near strawberries, tomatoes, cucumbers, and squash adds trace minerals to soil. This helps to boost the disease resistance of the nearby plants and deters tomato worms.
- Alfalfa planted with lettuce and beans adds nitrogen, iron, potassium, and phosphorous to the soil.
- When sweet alyssum is planted with broccoli, eggplant, corn, potatoes, and beans, it attracts hoverflies and wasps that eat aphids.
- Not only is the nasturtium flower beautiful, but when planted near radishes, cucumbers, fruit trees, and cabbage, it also detracts whiteflies, squash bugs, and cucumber beetles. In addition, aphids will dine on the nasturtium petals instead of the fruit trees.
- Marigolds may well be the superheroes of any edible garden. They make gorgeous bouquets of cut flowers and can be planted next to almost any flower or

to create a more tightly knit sense of community by opening it up and using it. The idea that more people will get outside and garden in the front yard is entirely plausible, especially in light of the interest in organic food. By now, even urban dwellers are growing their own lettuce, tomatoes, and peas in pots on rooftops, in sun-filled spaces, and in front yards. If you're an organic produce eater like me, it is the freshest, most nutritious food you will ever eat. Plus, the time you spend gardening gets you outside, which means you're not using the interior utilities. The big bonus for the environment is that the food you grow doesn't cause any pollution in transportation. We also hope that someone who is going to eat

Photo by Roy Yerushalmi.

herb to release a substance that repels root-feeding nematodes. They also keep whiteflies away from tomatoes.

If you are planting an herb garden, make sure it is close to the kitchen so the herbs will be readily available when you need them.

WHAT MAKES THIS HOME GREEN?

The founders of the renowned plant-based diet brand Forks Over Knives, Darshana Thacker and Brian Wendel, are absolute dream clients. Since they're vegan chefs, they didn't need much convincing when it came to implementing sustainable elements in their home design. To say the

kitchen is the centerpiece of this home would be an understatement!

Because they don't cook with oil and need a really great system to steam and sauté, their kitchen required more cooktop burners than the average household. We were able to skip a bulky ventilation system, usually seen hanging over the cooktop, because Darshana doesn't cook with any oils. More steam exhaust means there's not as much noxious smoke coming back into the environment. Which is a great bonus! Streamlined vent hoods on either side of the burners work sufficiently for them. They also contribute aesthetically to the open design plan connecting the dining and living room areas to the kitchen and the backyard, where they have a robust herb and vegetable garden.

FORKS OVER KNIVES

Photos by Roy Yerushalmi

NOISE POLLUTION

If an outdoor space is to flow with the interiors, in addition to being aesthetically pleasing and functioning well, it must be protected from unwanted noise. It's nearly impossible to create an indoor-outdoor flow, or even keep windows open, when you hear unpleasant noises outside, like vehicles, other people, helicopters, and barking dogs. The two best ways to combat exterior noise are running water and massive numbers of plants, trees, or shrubs.

Exterior fountains and ponds are also noisy, but the sound the water makes is a pleasant one. Fountains and ponds with small waterfalls incorporated between the noise and living areas will help create a more peaceful environment. They may also attract small animals looking for water, so plan accordingly.

LIGHTING POLLUTION

If you live in the country, you have a pleasure most urban and suburban folks do not get to enjoy each evening: a view of the stars. But light "pollution" has negative effects beyond not being able to see stars. The light that escapes from our buildings and exterior landscapes alters human sleep patterns, plant growth, and wildlife behavior.

To help combat the problem, install energy-efficient lighting with motion sensors that have fixtures to prevent light from exiting out above the fixture. The International Dark-Sky Association actually provides a manufacturer's directory with a list of approved light fixtures (www.darksky.org).

Lush trees, hedges, shrubs, and vines planted on the border of a property also serve to diminish unwanted noise. The thicker the planting, the more noise will be blocked. Additionally, trees, hedges, shrubs, and vines provide privacy, security, and safety.

OUTDOOR KITCHENS

Whenever possible, include an outdoor area for cooking. There must be something in our DNA that attracts us to places where food is cooking. Most

Photo by Erika Bierman.

parties wind up in the kitchen, and an outdoor "kitchen" is no exception. Preparing and grilling food outside has three primary benefits.

First, since most people cook outside when it is warm, doing so saves energy and reduces the burden on the utilities when air-conditioning loads are probably highest. Second, there is always less cleanup when food is prepared on a grill. Less cleanup means you use less water, energy, and other resources. Third, food takes on a whole new flavor and feel when it is prepared (and hopefully eaten) outside. The variety in dining experience brought on by a cookout seems to make people really happy.

8

BEDROOMS AND NURSERIES

Even the most experienced practitioner will find it nearly impossible to make a home completely green. Some factors pertaining to building or remodeling structures are simply out of your control. You have even less control over your environment when you go to work, the gym, shopping, or traveling.

There is one area of the home, however, in which you can take control by concentrating your green efforts: the bedroom. Since most of us spend a third of our lives in the bedroom of our home, it makes sense to make it the greenest and healthiest room of the home. The eight hours we spend sleeping each night is a vulnerable time for our bodies to literally regenerate.

When you sleep, your brain is creating hormones like melatonin that help fight diseases. A space that has clean air, plenty of sunlight during the day and darkness during the night, nontoxic furniture,

Photo by R. Zamani.

environmentally sound materials, and a void of hazardous electromagnetic fields gives the body the best chance to recuperate from the poisons we encounter on a daily basis.

A nontoxic bedroom is even more crucial for infants and children, who, pound for pound, are much more susceptible to the dangerous chemicals found in most conventional furniture, fabrics, and finish materials. Unfortunately, most parents don't realize this when they set up nurseries for a newborn or decorate spaces for their children. With the best intentions, they rush out and purchase new flooring, paint, furniture, accessories, toys, mattresses, and linens.

If the materials aren't green, chances are the room is flooded with toxic off-gassing. To make matters worse, parents often close all the windows so the

Photo by Erika Bierman.

Photo by R. Zamani.

"We do not inherit the earth from our ancestors; we borrow it from our children."

—Native American Proverb

child won't "catch a draft." It's a perfect storm of chemicals inundating the infant or child, who has an already-compromised immune system.

WALL AND CEILING MATERIALS

All surface materials should be nontoxic. Use no-VOC paints, healthy wall covering, or earth plaster. None of these products should release harmful chemicals into the bedroom or nursery.

If humidity levels are a concern, consider breathable surfaces like earth plaster for its ability to absorb and release moisture as needed. Regulating the humidity levels will also reduce the need for a humidifier, which could present its own health problems. Unless the water cartridges of humidifiers are routinely cleaned with peroxide, they are breeding grounds for microbial growth. When you combine dirty humidifiers with carpets or rugs and closed windows, you are certain to have a proliferation of bacterial growth. Contrary to popular opinion, you want to keep humidifiers out of infant rooms.

FRESH AIR AND NATURAL LIGHT

Bedrooms should have operable windows that allow plenty of air and natural light into the room. Even in the colder months, fresh air needs to circulate in a room. Especially in an infant's room, there needs to be an abundance of oxygen. Having the space too tightly sealed is not an optimal condition for brain development.

Ceiling fans in conjunction with open windows really aid in bringing air circulation into the space. UV rays from the sun act as a natural disinfectant. At least once daily open the windows and window coverings to allow the elements to come in and toxins to leave. The UV rays act as a disinfectant, the air is able to circulate, and natural light creates a far superior environment for playing, reading, or resting.

ELECTRONICS

Less is more in a bedroom. Bau-biologists believe that electromagnetic fields (EMFs) can compromise

human health. EMFs are man-made radiation from man-made electrical current. The AC current comes from electronics like clocks and televisions, and the DC current occurs when metal, like the coils in conventional box springs, become magnetized.

An actual, measurable, low level of electrical current is stored, concentrated, and radiates from the metal coils and throws off the human body's own natural, magnetic field. It affects our cells' ability to communicate with each other and can cause changes in functions of cells and tissues. It does sound a little sci-fi, but when you wake from a night of tossing and turning, feeling fatigued, it may well be the EMFs negatively affecting you. More serious side effects include decreases in melatonin, alterations of the immune system, accelerated tumor growth, changes in biorhythms, and changes in brain activity and heart rate.

There are two ways to reduce the problem: remove electronics from the bedroom and do not sleep in beds or mattresses which contain metal. Choose battery-operated alarm clocks, sound machines, and any other device that is close to your head. Do not locate a home office in the bedroom.

Keep cell phone chargers, printers, and computers out of the bedroom. As crazy as it sounds, televisions should not be in bedrooms either. Reserve the Netflix and chilling for living rooms! Steer clear of electric blankets by dressing warmer or adding more blankets. In an infant's room remove the monitor from the crib and place it on the dresser at least three feet from the baby. It will still effectively pick up sound.

MATTRESSES, PILLOWS, AND TOPPERS

Select natural-fiber pillows and mattresses. Most mattresses are treated with fire retardant chemicals like polybrominated diphenyl ethers (PBDEs). This carcinogen accumulates in humans who are exposed to it and can cause breast cancer and irregular brain development in children. Replace commercial mattresses with natural fiber mattresses. Chemical-free wool is a natural fire retardant that won't harm you.

Most foam pillows are sprayed with flame retardants known to cause irreversible damage to children's nervous systems. Unless otherwise stated, foam is generally made from petrochemicals, which off-gas chemicals throughout the night, right into your face, mouth, nose, throat, and skin. Synthetic pillows also have a higher percentage of dust mites found in the dense coarse foam material. Down or feather pillows, sometimes believed to cause allergies, are actually better solutions, as the tightly woven fabric used to contain feathers and down acts as a barrier to keep dust mites out of the pillow.

Human beings sweat during the night, about a pint per night on average. This is a natural way to release toxins in the body. But these fluids go right into the pillow and mattress. The trapped moisture, chemicals, fire retardants, and poly foam materials are a conducive environment for microbial growth and dust mites. Protect pillows, mattresses, duvets, and blankets with natural fiber covers that can be washed regularly. Wool mattress toppers covered in organic cotton wick away moisture and can be washed easily and regularly.

In infant rooms, it is especially important to buy organic fiber mattress pads and mattresses with no metal coils. First, doing so eliminates low-level fields of electric radiation. Second, vomit, urine, and drool combined with the plastic of commercial mattresses create supercharged bacteria.

Underdeveloped immune and endocrine systems are compromised in this situation. Recently, studies have supported the belief that SIDS is a side effect of a toxic mattress. For the same reason, mattresses shouldn't be stored in the garage. Carbon monoxide from car exhaust concentrates in mattresses, which can poison an infant when they breathe the fumes. To keep a mattress free of moisture, use a double layer of a wool mattress pad, a naturally fire-retardant material, and then a tightly fitted sheet. Wash them at least once a week.

They say you can't machine wash and dry down because it becomes damaged. We suggest machine washing and drying down comforters and pillows with nontoxic cleaning products once a season. We've been doing this for years and are at a loss as to when this "damage" is going to occur. If it's at all possible, bring your pillows and blankets and wool toppers outside to air in the sun at least once a month. The sun is a natural disinfectant. If you live in a building with no place to do this, place your bedding in front of an open window in the direct sunlight.

At least every few months, or any time someone has been sick with a cold, it is a good idea to throw the pillows and duvets/blankets in the washing machine on the gentle cycle with an environmentally friendly laundry detergent.

BEDS AND CHILDREN'S FURNITURE

In the bedroom, use furniture that is made from FSC-certified or reclaimed solid woods attached with eco-friendly binders and finished with nontoxic materials. Fabrics, padding, and cushions should be made of organic, durable, and easy-to-clean materials. This chapter will concentrate on resources for healthy bed frames and children's furniture, which is generally located in children's bedrooms. For a more complete list of furniture resources, refer to chapter 2, "Furniture and Accessories."

Bed frames should be raised above the floor and constructed with slats that allow air to flow under mattresses and provide enough support to eliminate the need for a box spring. Bed frames should be constructed of solid wood and contain no metal.

Nontoxic finishes for cribs are mandatory because teething infants often chew on the rails to relieve pain. FSC wood, no-VOC paint, and nontoxic sealer make cribs safe for a little one who is teething.

This serene space invites you to a sound sleep, especially when the mattress is made of latex and organic wool toppers. (Photo by Mark Tanner.)

BEDDING AND TOWELS

When nonorganic bed linens and towels are finished and sent to you, there are still trace amounts of toxic pesticide residues on the fabrics, which you absorb through your skin while you sleep and dry yourself after bathing. Formaldehyde, classified as a human carcinogen linked to brain and lung cancer and leukemia, is the ingredient that makes most sheets stain resistant and wrinkle free. Many towels are treated with triclosan, a chemical antibacterial agent. This is overkill, and it promotes superbacteria. Bamboo towels don't need any additional chemicals because bamboo has natural antibacterial properties, and it can thrive without any pesticides.

Most commercial sheets and towels are made of conventional cotton, which uses a disproportionate amount of pesticides and herbicides in its cultivation. The chemicals seep into the ground and bodies of water, contaminating them and harming humans, fish, and wildlife. There are entire villages in China who suffer from cancer as a result of this same type of pollution in their water supplies.

To create a healthier local and global environment, purchase organic bedding and towels. Organic fibers don't have toxic finishes, and the more they are washed, the softer they become, without polluting your bedroom and the world. Bedding should always be cleaned with perfume-free and phosphate-free biodegradable detergents.

Every surface in this green showcase bedroom was covered with an eco-friendly surface. The carpet, by Bentley Prince Street, is made of recycled material and is recyclable. Wall cover by Innovations is from their Environments line. Furniture is from Mitchell Gold, a longtime champion of earth-friendly manufacturing. The bedding, by Anna Sova, is made of organic cotton, as are the curtains. And a sustainable succulent!

An FSC-certified, AFM-Safecoat-stained four-poster bed creates a room within a room in this spectacular master suite designed for a hip young couple. Having triumphed over childhood cancer, the husband required a space that tread lightly on the planet and went easy on his immune system. Organic hotel linens

Photo by Mark Tanner.

Bedroom by Lori Dennis. Photo by Ken Hayden.

by Lori Dennis, hand-scooped bamboo floors, and organic linen curtain fabric help create a sanctuary that soothes the body and considers the environment.

Organic Bed Linens, Towel Sources, and Shower Curtains

Pottery Barn (www.potterybarn.com) has great style, there's no way around it. Their organic sheet and towel collections come in a variety of bold stripes, solids, flannels, botanicals, and hotel-style linens. They can be monogrammed for that custom touch.

Coyuchi (www.coyuchi.com) sells beautiful heirloom-quality bedding products for adults and children made from certified organic cotton or wool. As the company became successful, the founder started giving back to the farmers who grew the organic and Fair Trade Certified cotton through a livestock charity. The Cow Project focuses on helping the farmers acquire livestock that contributes to the well-being of their families and farms. The manure and urine from these cows are collected for organic fertilizer and pesticides, and milk provides additional nutrition for the villagers. The cows are respected, well treated, and loved by their owners.

Rawganique (www.rawganique.com) sells sweatshop-free, certified-organic hemp and linen products made in the United States, Europe, and Canada. The company carries the world's first and only organically grown hemp towels, pure and sustainable as they come. They offer fine French linen sheets made without chemical finishes, heavy dyes, or toxic finishes at half the cost of competitors.

Instead of cheap PVC shower curtains that off-gas toxins and need frequent replacement, buy hemp shower curtains—many of the vendors we listed above are great sources to shop for sustainable shower curtains. For under a hundred dollars, you will get a curtain that will last a lifetime. Hemp, used for ship's sails, is water resistant and extremely durable. Most of them are pretty plain; they look like unfinished painting canvases.

AREA RUGS

Wood floors, covered with area rugs, are the best for the bedrooms. Wood floors are softer than stone or tile, and area rugs help accomplish that cozy feeling that is so desirable in a bedroom. It is especially important to frequently clean area rugs in bedrooms and nurseries, more so than other rooms of the house. Because you spend the most time in these rooms, more accumulation of dead human and pet cells, hair, dust, and dander settles in these spaces. Without frequently cleaning, you are basically providing a free buffet for bacteria and dust mites.

Avoid using new wall-to-wall carpet or synthetic area rugs in children's rooms. A child who plays on a synthetic rug is extremely susceptible to the harmful chemicals that off-gas into the room. Parents are afraid their toddlers will get hurt on wood floors, but a few childhood bumps are a rite of passage that teaches humans how to balance and avoid falling. Poisonous chemical carpeting is the furthest thing from providing a safe environment for your child to grow.

Particularly troublesome are wall-to-wall carpets that can never be removed or cleaned properly. As these carpets get older, they have unavoidable dust mites and microbes proliferating in them. Alternative materials like bamboo, wool, organic cotton, vintage rags, nontoxic rubber mats, and eco-friendly, replaceable floor tiles are much, much better solutions for removable rugs in bedrooms.

This chapter will focus on rugs for children's rooms. Please refer to chapter 2, "Furniture and Accessories," for additional rug sources.

Letting a child's imagination run wild doesn't mean sacrificing safety or health. In this fire engine station of a bedroom, recycled tire flooring cushions daring jumps from the top of the engine, and low-VOC paint reduces toxic fumes. (At the time we designed this room, darker colors were not readily available in no-VOC paints. Today you have a much, much wider variety of available and affordable no-VOC colors.) Anna Sova organic linens ensure a restful night.

Photo by Christian Romero.

- **Floor Score** (www.floorscore.com) sells about ten different styles of rubber flooring tiles. They are made from recycled tires, come in a wide selection of colors, and are easy to install.
- **VivaTerra** (www.vivaterra.com) sells naturally antibacterial bamboo rugs in three earthy colors and multiple sizes.
- **Flokati** (www.flokati.com) has a large collection of natural wool rugs in many colors, sizes, and patterns. They're great for kids' rooms because they can be thrown in a commercial washing machine or shaken outdoors and left in the sunlight to disinfect.

- **FLOR** (www.flor.com), known for bold, colorful rug tiles, is a perfect solution for kids' rooms. Tiles are easily replaced when soiled or destroyed, eliminating the need to replace an entire carpet.

WINDOW TREATMENTS

Research indicates that a bedroom should be pitch black as you're drifting off to sleep, as light pollution cuts down on the production of melatonin. Wood and bamboo blinds work well in bedrooms because they block light and are easily cleaned. Fabric window coverings have the advantage of keeping the room warmer in winter months and potentially pitch black when blackout liners are added—but they are more difficult to clean.

When selecting fabric treatments, avoid materials treated with harmful chemical finishes. (These are usually added to make curtains hang straight without wrinkles.) Instead, select washable curtains made from organic fibers, which are easy to remove and replace.

(See chapter 3, "Fabrics and Window Treatments.")

Air Purifiers

It's so important to sleep with an air purifier every night. Sleeping is when your cells regenerate, and you'll want to give your cells the best chance to recuperate and rejuvenate. We have, in fact, done our research and discovered the best air purifiers for your home. Our recommendations are, however, on the expensive side. But read on because we'll save you the research and wasted money buying inexpensive filters that won't actually do a great job purifying the air. Bite the bullet and buy the best out there. This is one area where buying new (or refurbished) and the best is always worth it:

- **IQAir (www.iqair.com).** Our top recommendation is the medical grade air purifier IQAir. It's so important to have clean air while you sleep, and this one does the trick. We'd really suggest going for gold here! IQAir is a heavy-duty filter that cleans the air room by room or even the whole house, depending on your needs and budget.
- **Molekule (www.molekule.com).** The next choice on the list is the Molekule. What sets the technology in the Molekule apart from others is that unlike most air filters, which merely capture and collect pollutants, the Molekule also destroys them. It's also a rather elegant-looking device, if we do say so!
- **Dyson (www.dyson.com).** Running about $365, the Dyson Pure Cool Link Desk Purifier is the least expensive one on our list that is still incredibly effective! The real selling point of this purifier is the portable size. It's great for desktops or laundry rooms.

9

GREEN BUILDING

Homes and offices account for about half of the energy use and greenhouse gas emissions worldwide. The traditional methods used to build and operate our homes contribute to smog, acid rain, and climate change.

Thankfully, there is now a growing interest in building and certifying structures that are less harmful to our environment and the people occupying these spaces. Rating systems like Energy Star and LEED are becoming more popular as people begin to realize the economic, environmental, and health benefits of building green structures. The less energy and raw materials that are used and the more efficient these buildings become, the less pollution they will generate.

WHAT IS A GREEN HOME?

A green home is one that uses fewer resources, less energy, and less water than a conventional home. It has better indoor air quality and is healthier for the people living in it. Green homes are also more durable and cost less money to operate. Over the last thirty years the average square footage of a house has gone from about 1,500 to nearly 2,500 square feet. That means a lot more energy is being used to light and operate the same single-family home.

With about a million new homes being built in the United States every year, an enormous amount of raw materials and energy is used, and millions of tons of waste are created. Most of these homes are not built efficiently, so the energy it takes to heat, cool, light, and power them is even more astounding.

For ecological and economic reasons, people are downsizing and building green. Many states, municipalities, and utilities offer incentives, tax breaks, and rebates to do this. Fortunately, this is resulting in more people in the building industry looking for products that contain recycled content, have a positive impact on indoor air quality, save energy and water, and are produced locally to reduce the environmental costs of transportation.

A reasonable concern for anyone building a home is whether it will cost more to go green. The answer is not necessarily. New technologies have opened the doors to more efficient and less wasteful buildings, and alternative energy has become less expensive and more accessible.

This chapter will help you locate various products and services that will help you and your building team find suitable resources for your green building venture.

SIZE AND STYLE

Make sure the square footage is not bigger than needed to avoid wasting materials, labor, and energy. Build only as big as you truly need. It's a simple fact: the bigger the structure, the more you impact the environment.

While it is important to build smaller, it is equally important to build smart. Good design is green design. You can have a quality project that is not green, but you cannot have a green project that is also not a quality project. You cannot specify materials just because they are efficient without considering how they work in the space effectively.

You would be wasting your efforts if you just make a list of green products and start dropping them into your plans without really considering how they will aesthetically affect the project. If a building is not beautiful and functional, you haven't done your job

"You can have a quality project that is not green, but you cannot have a green project that is also not a quality project."

—ASID Regreen Program

and, worse, you risk it having to be remodeled shortly after you're gone. This is a good way to ruin your reputation and waste money, time, and resources. And wasting anything in this process is the polar opposite of what we are trying to accomplish.

SITE

Green building from the ground up or remodeling existing structures will require the efforts of an entire team of building professionals. Careful planning from the beginning stages can help reduce some of your carbon footprint in this process. Begin with site location (for new construction). Choose a site that is close to public transportation or services you will use daily. Contrary to popular belief, selecting a site in an urban area, one where you can walk or ride your bike to public transportation, work, shopping, recreation, and entertainment is green.

Locate or redesign the building and surrounding landscaping so that it takes advantage of what the climate has to offer.

If you have the opportunity to reuse a building, take it. Especially in a run-down, urban center, adaptively rehabilitating historic buildings is one of the most sustainable actions you can take. Many cities have urban revitalization programs and offer incentives to update these buildings. When you add green to your agenda, you can bet your project is slated for a home run.

After the project site is known, the next consideration is deconstruction. Notice we did not say demolition. The difference is using an informed labor force to assist in preserving all the materials they can. Bricks, lumber, salvaged architectural materials, doors, knobs, sinks, and almost every material you can think of can be diverted from landfills and recycled or reused in your project. Dispose of waste from construction using an eco-friendly approach instead of using landfills as your "go-to" option.

Landfills are bloated with waste, and incinerating construction waste creates air pollution. Both of these methods disregard the value of lost resources. Work with your team to think of every way you can minimize construction waste. Be resourceful by doing things like moving the old kitchen cabinets to the garage for storage. Sorting for salvage, recycling, and donation should become routine on a green construction site. You can contact your municipal recycling facility for the best options in your area. The goal is to keep as much out of the trash as possible.

If the soil is being displaced during construction, limit vegetation from being removed to help prevent soil erosion. Collect any soil that is removed during construction and reuse it in areas that will be landscaped. When they built the Getty Center in Los Angeles, one of the conditions was that all of the dirt that was dug out for foundation had to be reused on the site. If they managed to rearrange tens of thousands of pounds of dirt, you can do it on your site too.

If you're going for LEED certification, site selection and demolition waste are two prerequisites. You will have to start thinking green at the very beginning.

Another dream by the beach! This one for a mysterious bachelor-playboy with unlimited funds, a well-stamped passport, and a license to kill: James Bond is the epitome of camp. (And the model for an ideal design client!) Using his highly romanticized nature as an inspirational springboard, we designed this "Bond at the Beach" project as though it were

Photos by Stephen Busken.

BOND AT THE BEACH

Photos by Stephen Busken

where James Bond might spend his downtime between serving Her Majesty's Secret Service.

WHAT MAKES THIS HOME GREEN?

This home is in a multifamily building—always more eco-friendly than a single family home. The building meets a number of sustainable criteria, including its HVAC systems and solar, electrical, and water usage. This building is also walkable to what little reliable public transportation LA has to offer. It's a hop, skip, and jump away from entertainment, work, shopping—everything!

One of the greenest and most efficient ways to live in Los Angeles: beat sitting in freeway traffic and live within walking distance of work. The halls include Interface carpet tiles—carbon-neutral flooring made from recycled materials. One building using their flooring offsets the equivalent carbon emissions of nine round-trip flights between New York and Paris! Koroseal wall covering adorns the walls. Koroseal makes sure to use the safest raw materials available with the lowest environmental impact, and they always recycle any waste. Their wall coverings cost very little energy to produce and are easily maintained.

The kitchen features Caesarstone counters and Energy Star appliances. And the cabinetry and flooring are FSC certified. Between the large windows letting in the sea breeze and ceiling fans, we nearly eliminated the need for AC.

The entire home features high-performance fabrics so they'll hold up against all the elements at the beach. And multiple rooms contain ecosmart fireplaces.

10

HOME OFFICES

FIVE TIPS FOR DESIGNING A GROOVY GREEN HOME OFFICE

1. Get Your Office Organized

Okay, before we can start, we must get you organized! You're ready to overhaul your home office with cohesive decor and a mixture of built-in storage solutions, but before you start anything, you'll want to go as paper free as possible. Sign up for e-payments online, scan and digitize your documents, digitize your signature, and so forth. Then we can begin thinking about what's left and what will realistically be added to your paper stash to design optimal storage solutions for your home office. See, you're already going green, and you haven't even started yet.

2. Go Bold in Your Design Decisions

Don't be afraid of bold color choices! Or patterns! We have fun with clients who want bright, bold wallpaper or electric wall color to keep them inspired all day long. This isn't the space for rest, this is the space to keep you inspired and mentally active.

3. Flow: Tips on Desks and Chairs

Seating is the key for comfort in a home office. You'll be spending a lot of time in office chairs, so choose desk and lounge seating that you can comfortably adjust positions in all day long. That's the key to a really good chair: when you initially sit down, you don't need to be comfortable *right* away—you need to be able to adjust positions and sink in comfortably over time. If that chair isn't right, it won't matter if it's a beautiful space or not!

One of the biggest mistakes we see homeowners make again and again is pushing all their furniture up against the wall. Give your home office a designer touch by floating your desk in the middle of the space. This also places the desk in a Godfather-esque position of power and is great for the overall chi (good flow) of the space. It is an office, after all; your desk should take front and center. How your home office seating placement functions is twofold: firstly, you're likely spending a lot of time at your desk, so you'll want a relaxing view. Facing windows always helps! By the same token, you don't want visitors to be distracted, so the placement of extra seating is directional and will tell them where to look. It also better optimizes the feng shui of the space by facing windows.

Photo by Erika Bierman.

4. Giving Your Eyes a Break

When it comes to lighting, rely first on your natural light since it's easiest on the eyes, then put any additional lighting like task lighting or chandeliers on dimmers so it's easier to transition from day to

Selamat sources sustainably managed materials like rattan, jute, FSC-certified teak, and mahogany and prioritizes the heritage, ecosystems, and economies of their skilled artisans. Pictured: Deco Side Chair (available via www.perigold.com), Morgan Desk (available via www.perigold.com), Edith Mirror (available via www.perigold.com), Scallop Pendant (available via www.perigold.com), and Palm Occasional Chair (available via www.shopcandelabra.com). (Photo courtesy of Selamat Designs, www.selamatdesigns.com.)

Photo by Ken Hayden.

night. Consider getting a screen protector for laptops or televisions. On the walls, include art you want to look at all day long, and give yourself something to look at that isn't a screen! In the vein of going green, consider including some fresh flowers or low-maintenance plants throughout the space that will help improve the air quality of the space.

5. Hide Electric Cables

This one is pretty self-explanatory: nothing ruins a beautiful room quite like our twenty-first-century technocomforts, but you want to hide electric cables and stow unsightly printers away with some chic built-in cabinetry or up against walls, behind larger furniture pieces like consoles and media cabinets.

Photo by Stephen Busken.

BUILDING DESIGN

Good green building design has an abundance of natural light and airflow. The success of these two elements largely depends on the design of your window, heating, and cooling systems.

Natural and Artificial Light

If you have the opportunity to decide where windows and doors will be, think about what rooms are being used during different times of the day. This is especially important in home offices if you work from home often. Your eyes need a break from staring at screens. Provide opportunities for plenty of natural daylight. Make sure that the natural light source coincides with the way the rooms are used, and allow for cross ventilation.

Natural light and a lot of windows are great ways to reduce ambient lighting in the day, but poorly designed placement of these windows can lead to overheating and excessive energy use for cooling. Make wise placement decisions like not placing the largest windows on the west side. They will receive sun during the hottest parts of the day, making cooling the space less efficient. Clerestory windows on the west side are a good option for extremely hot climates where you want natural light in the afternoon to evening.

Provide an appropriate mix of ambient and task lighting. During the daylight hours, if possible, make sure all ambient lighting is provided by natural daylight. When daylight is unavailable, try solar tubes. Solar tubes and skylights reduce dependence on artificial light sources on sunny days and are a good way to get natural light into rooms with no windows, like hallways and laundry rooms. If the solar tubes are equipped with fluorescent fixtures, they will function as lights in the evening.

For nighttime, use the most energy-efficient lighting possible. Indirect fluorescent lighting is effective and has come a long way in its color quality. For task lighting, good choices are direct sources from compact fluorescents and LED light fixtures. Here are a couple of our favorites:

Solatube (www.solatube.com) is the world's leading manufacturer of tubular skylights, offering the highest-performance products in the industry.

Solar Track (www.solar-track.com) offers both skylights and solar tubes that track the sun (for maximum exposure in mornings and evenings) and are photovoltaic powered.

Operable windows are an essential component of natural airflow and light. The key is to make sure the windows you choose are energy efficient. There is no blanket remedy for choosing the right window. There are four Energy Star climate zones in North America: Northern Climate (Minneapolis, MN) which requires mostly heating; the North-Central (Washington, DC) and South-Central (Phoenix, AZ), which require heating and cooling; and the Southern Climate (Miami, FL), which requires mostly cooling. Depending on where the project is, you will have different needs.

The Efficient Windows Collaborative (EWC) is a member organization with a great website to help you with your choices. The site provides unbiased information on the benefits of energy-efficient windows, descriptions of how they work, and recommendations for selection and use. This site is easy to use and has a thorough list of eco-friendly vendors for windows and skylights.

Another bonus is that it provides detailed information on how to get monetary compensation for homeowners who install energy-efficient windows. Any time you can show a client how to save money, you help enforce why design professionals are necessary. (www.efficientwindows.org).

There are many technical facts about selecting windows with good energy performance. You can begin by looking at the Energy Star ratings. Some of the other universal elements of efficient windows are multiglazing layers (triple is the best), low-conductivity gas fills, seals on insulated units, heat-reflective (low-emissivity) coatings, multiple low-e coatings, advanced weather stripping, and new frame systems. Exterior shading can also play a role. It is best to work with a trusted local window professional for site-specific fenestration decisions.

There is a debate about whether plastic or wood windows are better for the environment. Most people think that wood is a better choice for the environment, but that may not be the case. Vinyl windows can be made of sustainable, environmentally friendly, low-maintenance materials that last for decades and do not emit toxins.

Wood windows tend to be less efficient and require more maintenance and faster replacements than plastic. Plastic windows come in both ABS and vinyl (PVC). ABS is a better choice. Windows made of ABS do not contain chlorine, so there is no risk of dioxin generation during an accidental fire or incineration at the end of the product's life.

When installing windows in wet areas like bathrooms, showers, or tubs, select a window that has a moisture-tolerant frame made of plastic or fiberglass. Metal or wood frames will break down when they come in contact with water on a daily basis. Sills must also be made of a surface that is impermeable to water and constructed as if it were on the exterior. Solid material sills are better than tiled surfaces. If you are going to use a tiled surface, however, use an epoxy grout.

Almost all North American window manufacturers are producing windows that are energy efficient as a result of legislation and consumer demand. Check with your preferred provider for the most sustainable offering they provide.

Natural and Artificial Ventilation, Heating, and Cooling

Use materials and methods that aid in the natural heating and cooling of the structure. "Build tight, ventilate right" is a common saying in green building. A tightly sealed home improves comfort and indoor air quality—as long as you have specified nontoxic surface materials and furnishings. When you seal holes and cracks in the home's envelope and in heating and cooling duct systems, you can reduce drafts, moisture, dust, pollen, and noise. In addition to using less energy because they don't have to work as hard, energy-efficient heating and air systems improve the overall comfort of a home. We know that proper window placement and type can help lessen the load on heating and cooling systems.

Ceiling Fans

Combine good design with ceiling fans to avoid using air-conditioning. If your climate is unforgiving and you do use air-conditioning, chose Energy Star–rated systems. They will reduce energy consumption by 20–40 percent over conventional units. Make sure to install programmable thermostats for both heating and cooling systems.

G Squared Art (www.g2art.com), a 1% for the Planet member, offers a unique ceiling fan line.

The Modern Fan Co. (www.modernfan.com) has an impressive selection of ceiling fans, and they offer color-corrected compact fluorescent–compatible fixtures.

Lamps Plus (www.lampsplus.com) has a wide selection of attractive ceiling fans that incorporate LED bulbs for maximum efficiency, like the one pictured that we added to a budget and family-friendly vacation rental property in Los Angeles.

Exhaust Fans

Exhaust fans are an important component in a tightly sealed building. Use them while cooking in the kitchen and showering/bathing in bathrooms if there are no windows. It is good green practice to design bathrooms with operable windows or good sources of ventilation to prevent mold growth.

For bathrooms with no windows, make sure to install a quiet and energy-efficient fan. Our favorites are from Panasonic (www.panasonic.com). They're quiet, efficient, and reliable, and they look good. Kitchen ventilation is equally as important, as you may recall from the appliances chapter.

Photo by Roy Yerushalm.

Radiant Heating

For heating a home, radiant heat has a number of advantages over forced air. It is more efficient than baseboard and forced air because no energy is lost when the heat rises. The lack of forced air is advantageous to people with allergies. Water-based systems (hydronic) use little electricity.

With radiant heat, unlike central air, you can zone different areas of the home for different temperatures. Radiant heating systems can be installed under most flooring: wood, concrete, stone, and tile. And there is more freedom in the interior design because you do not have to consider the placement of vents. If you're working on a tight budget (and who isn't?) and you can't afford radiant heating throughout the interior, consider at least putting it in the bathrooms.

If you have forced air for cooling and heating, consider mechanical, whole-house filtration systems or, at the very least, filters on your heating intakes, the furnace itself, and vents to each room. Some air quality specialists recommend a "bake off" after new construction or a remodel to speed up the off-gassing of chemicals in the residence.

Plan to vacate the house for a few days, turn the temperature and airflow up higher than usual, open all the windows and continue for at least three days. This is said to help release the toxic chemicals faster and make the air cleaner to breathe when you finally occupy the space.

Finally, make sure the garage is sealed off from the rest of the house. Toxic fumes from cars are the last thing you want seeping into your home.

11

CLEANING AND MAINTAINING INTERIORS AND LANDSCAPES

The two major factors concerning cleaning and maintenance of interiors and landscapes are toxic products and waste. We've spent nine chapters learning how to design and furnish properties in a more sustainable and healthy manner. To turn around and drench them in toxic products on a weekly basis would be counterproductive to the green foundation we've laid.

By this point, we also realize that landfill space is scarce and expensive. The less we throw away, the less we need to be concerned with poisoning our environment, finding new places to dump trash, and wasting valuable resources. Eco-friendly maintenance of the interior and landscape helps to reduce the negative aspects these activities have on the environment. This chapter will go into detail about green cleaning methods and products, recycling, hazardous waste disposal, and outdoor maintenance.

To ensure that the home you've designed is run properly after you have gone, it is always a good idea to make a maintenance binder with specific details about the home, including water, gas, and electrical supply shutoff locations, how to operate automated and low-voltage systems, and relevant information from this chapter.

START AT THE FRONT DOOR

Place good, old-fashioned welcome mats at all the entries to the home. Use track-off mats at the entries of buildings to reduce indoor pollution. While this is a great idea (and who doesn't love a nice welcome mat?), an even better option is to remove your shoes when you enter a residence. This simple act helps to reduce the amount of pesticides and chemicals that accumulate on the soles of our shoes and then get tracked all over our indoor space. A way to encourage people to perform this act without having to ask is to design for seating, shoe, and slipper storage near an entry to the home.

CLUTTER

Fires are one of the most toxic events that can occur in a residence. Do everything you can to prevent fires, including installing smoke detectors, replacing batteries as needed, and installing sprinklers. An effective and less-expensive fire-prevention technique is to avoid clutter. Make sure to remove clutter by anything hot that can ignite, like ovens, furnaces, and space heaters.

Less clutter also means less dust, which requires fewer cleaning products and less water. We're not a big fan of dust-collecting objects. Open spaces allow for fresh air to circulate, and this makes a room feel more inviting. If someone does have a collection, make sure it is displayed in a closed glass or Lucite case/cabinet; this will help eliminate most of the dust that a collection can collect.

CLEANING SUPPLIES

Organic cleaners are made mostly of plant-based materials. Synthetic cleaners are often made from petroleum-based products. Petroleum-based products are toxic, and when they are rinsed down the drain, they wind up in our waterways and oceans. If you like eating fish, you may want to begin using nontoxic cleaning products.

Furniture and finish materials also contribute to poor indoor air quality, which negatively affects our health. Conventional cleaning products, reintroduced to the home on a weekly basis, however, may be the biggest culprits. There are thousands of chemicals used in American cleaning products and new ones added each year. It is impossible to keep track of them all.

Frequently, the EPA doesn't test chemicals in these products for human safety. Sometimes it takes decades of proof that a product is deadly before it is removed from production in the United States. Currently there are thousands of harmful chemicals in conventional cleaners that are being used every day. Replacing toxic cleaners with healthier options might be one of the easiest ways to literally clean up our act.

How to Make a Homemade Nontoxic All-Purpose Cleaner

With a few simple, natural ingredients, you can have nontoxic cleaners that will work throughout the entire house in just five minutes.

Ingredients and materials:
- One cup distilled water
- One cup distilled white vinegar
- Half a lemon, juiced
- 10–15 drops of essential oils (dealer's choice on the scent that's most soothing to you!)
- Spray bottle

Instructions: Simply combine all the liquid in the bottle and shake! And voilà, you're good to go with a sustainable, nontoxic cleaner for all your surfaces and minor rug spills. If you don't have the five minutes to spare, nontoxic cleaning products are just as easy to buy these days.

Keeping a clean and green house doesn't have to be expensive or a bother. Many cleaning products are already in your house and ready to be used. Dr. Bronner's Pure-Castile Soap, baking soda, white vinegar, spray bottles, and hand towels can be your complete cleaning arsenal.

As simple as it sounds, water, vinegar, baking soda, hydrogen peroxide, lemon, cheap vodka, vegetable oils, and rags from old towels, T-shirts, diapers, and socks can take care of most of the cleaning needs throughout a home. Buying a few spray bottles for each concoction and using these ingredients to clean will save the environment from having to deal with millions of plastic bottles from production to transportation to disposal.

Vinegar is a superpower when it comes to healthy cleaning. It has natural antibacterial properties, so it works as a beneficial disinfectant. Vinegar will clean most surfaces, but do not use it on limestone or marble because it may dissolve them. Make sure that the vinegar you are using is not made from petroleum sources. There should be an identifying label that says "made from grain" on the bottle.

Baking soda is also an all-around cleaner, which acts as a mild abrasive when mixed with water or an odor absorber when placed in the refrigerator, freezer, or bottom of a trash can.

While there are greener products on the market, for the times when you need something a little bit stronger, we recommend Murphy Oil Soap and Bon Ami Powder Cleanser. Murphy Oil Soap is a miracle cleaner and one of our all-time favorites. It gently cleans almost any surface and smells great. When you need super scrubbing power, try Bon Ami Powder Cleanser, a great substitute for chlorine-based Ajax or Comet.

Any time you can skip water, rags, and cleaning products by using a vacuum to suck up dirt, do it. It will use fewer resources and less energy.

Cleaning Products: Reading the Package

If you're uncertain if something is okay to use, check for this wording on packages: phosphate-free, vegetable-oil-based, no dyes, fragrance-free, biodegradable, non-petroleum-based. If you can purchase cleaners in a bulk size and refill smaller containers, it saves the need to extract materials, manufacture, and then dispose of them.

BATHROOMS

White vinegar and baking soda are really all you need to clean a bathroom that has just been installed or remodeled. After dust and hair are wiped or swept up, vinegar and baking soda will do most of the work. If you don't like the smell of vinegar, don't worry; it doesn't smell after it dries.

Toilet bowls can be cleaned with two cups of white vinegar (allow to sit for a few minutes) and baking soda and a good scrubbing.

For shiny faucets, wipe them down with vinegar, follow up with a clean rag, and wipe on a drop of oil to keep them shiny longer. Mineral deposits on faucets can be removed by soaking a rag in vinegar and allowing it to sit on the faucets for an hour.

For rust on any porcelain—sinks, tubs, toilets—use vinegar on a rag to wipe off.

When you want to regain that out-of-the-box sparkle, cheap vodka will produce a reflective shine on any metal or mirrored surfaces. Vodka has no color or smell and is a lot less toxic than rubbing alcohol.

Clogs are usually caused by hair and grease. Of course, preventing these items from going down drains will aid in the elimination of clogs in the first place. If you do get a clog, try pouring baking soda and vinegar down the drain followed by boiling hot water. If that doesn't work, call a plumber to snake the drain. Do not use harsh chemical products; they are unnecessary, and they are bad for your health, indoor air quality, the drains, and the aquatic life at the other end of their journey.

Instead of using artificial air fresheners, releasing harmful VOCs into the air, place fragrant plants like lavender, mint, basil, or rosemary in the bathroom. A trick that always eliminates a stinky smell immediately is lighting a match.

In addition to helping eliminate bad smells, exhaust fans should be used when showering or bathing to prevent mold and mildew. Or, if you have a window in the bathroom, make sure to open it when the bathroom is steamy for mold and mildew prevention. Ventilate for about fifteen minutes after the bathroom has become steamy.

Practice water conservation in the room that uses the most fresh water in the house. Don't use the toilet as an ashtray or wastebasket. Turn off the water while brushing teeth, shaving, and soaping. If cold water will do, avoid using hot water. And take shorter showers.

QUICK TIPS FOR CLEANING KITCHENS

Try to use the garbage disposal as little as possible by adding leftover food to a compost pail. If you do use your disposal, keep it clean with ice and a leftover lemon.

If the drain becomes clogged, use the same trick as in the bathroom. Pour baking soda and white vinegar down the drain, and, after a half hour, pour boiling hot water down the drain.

It uses less water to run a full load of dishes than hand-washing them. Adding white vinegar in the rinse dispenser of the machine will make dishes sparkle and eliminate the need for a harsh chemical rinsing agent.

To wash the dishwasher, place a bowl with about two cups of white vinegar in the bottom of the dishwasher and run it without any additional cleaner.

Don't put wood in the dishwasher. This means knives, bowls, and cutting boards. It will dry them out, and they will crack and be destroyed. In this case, you will have to clean and dry these items by hand. Make sure to clean cutting boards in cold water—hot water sets in odors. Follow with a thin layer of inexpensive vegetable oil every fourth time they are washed.

The best advice on keeping sinks clean is to wipe up food and sauces before they stain. Baking soda or Bon Ami combined with scrubbing action will clean the sink without damaging it.

This same advice is used for the stove and oven. Spills and splatters should be wiped up immediately after the hot surface cools. This will eliminate the need for harsh chemical cleaners to clean caked-on substances. Never use oven cleaner. Most are made with a chemical called sodium hydroxide. In addition to being extremely dangerous to breathe, the noxious chemicals seep into the earth and waterways when rags or paper towels are cleaned or disposed of. For extremely filthy grills, let them sit in a gallon of water and one cup of baking soda overnight.

If raw meat juice has contaminated a surface, spray it with vinegar followed by hydrogen peroxide for a harmless germ-killing solution.

Tomato paste is a gentle polish for copper pots. To remove tarnish, dip them in boiling vinegar and wipe dry with a cloth. A salt and lemon scrub works too.

To clean silver, use nontoxic, biodegradable polish. If you can't find one, line a sink or bowl with aluminum foil and pour in boiling water and a few tablespoons each of salt and baking soda. Allow to sit for ten minutes, and then remove and polish with a dry, soft cloth. Repeat if necessary. But be aware that you must hand-wash these items forever after because they tarnish to a yellow color if cleaned in a dishwasher.

Clean coffee makers and teakettles with vinegar and water. In coffee makers, run a few cycles of vinegar water through the machine. To remove mineral buildup from teakettles, boil vinegar and water for a half hour, and polish the outside with a baking-soda-and-vinegar paste.

Use unbleached wax paper, which is biodegradable, instead of plastic wrap.

If you use paper napkins, buy recycled products, and recycle in a compost pail. It's really best to use cloth napkins over and over and over and over again.

Skip paper towels for cleaning spills and opt for dish towels instead.

Turn on vents when cooking to keep the house clean and smoke out of the lungs.

Follow these tips for conserving water:

- Operate the dishwasher only with a full load.
- Scrape, don't rinse, dishes before they are loaded into the dishwasher.
- Buy a water-efficient dishwasher.
- Don't run hot water to thaw food.
- Store drinking water in the refrigerator instead of letting the water run to cool.

KEEPING SURFACES SHINY!

Countertops, windows, mirrors, and showers can be cleaned with a mix of equal portions of vinegar and warm water in a spray bottle. Add a few drops of tea tree oil or lavender for a fragrant smell.

Dust regularly. Doing so eliminates buildup of allergens.

Sweep, vacuum, and mop floors weekly. Fill a basin or bucket with cold water, add the appropriate amount of cleaner, put rags in, wring them out until they are damp, and mop away. Change rags as they accumulate too much dirt. If you have a normal amount of traffic and the floors are being swept, vacuumed, and wet mopped once a week, these rags shouldn't be too dirty.

For no-wax floors, mop with one cup of vinegar for every gallon of water. (On laminate wood, use a half-cup for every gallon.) If the manufacturer states you shouldn't use vinegar, then don't. Use Murphy Oil Soap instead.

For glazed tile and stone floors, mop with a half cup of baking soda to one gallon of water, wash, and rinse.

Most new floors don't require wax. Their finishes are long lasting and protective. If you have an older floor that requires wax, begin with a clean floor and apply an organic wax. Less-trafficked areas probably only require a small amount of wax once or twice a year. Areas that are seldom walked on (under the furniture, close to walls) probably only need waxing once every few years.

MOLD AND MILDEW

The key to preventing mildew and mold is good ventilation. If you do spot mildew, attack it immediately with a spray made of two cups of water and one-quarter teaspoon each of tea tree oil and lavender. Shake first and spray everywhere. The oils will do the work for you; there's no need to wipe.

Mold can be sprayed with straight white vinegar and wiped off. The use of a dehumidifier in humid climates can help eliminate mold and mildew, keeping it out of the air and off of your things. In humid weather, empty the drip pan and wipe it clean daily. Once a week, clean the water bucket with a natural cleanser or a spray of white vinegar followed by a spray of hydrogen peroxide and wipe clean.

FURNITURE AND AREA RUGS

White canvas slipcovers are one of our favorite upholstery treatments. The fact that you can just toss them in the washer when they are dirty is a dream. Clean all light-colored fabrics—slipcovers, towels, sheets, and so forth—with hydrogen- or oxygen-based bleaches instead of chlorine-based bleach. Chlorine has been tied to breast cancer and wreaks all kinds of havoc on marine life when it eventually winds up in the ocean.

Leather can be cleaned and oiled with liquid saddle soap. Leather furniture can be oiled with inexpensive vegetable oil.

Don't use artificial furniture polish. It contains flammable and toxic chemicals that might smell nice but nonetheless are polluting the indoor and outdoor environment. Instead, use natural-based polishes or vegetable oil. Two parts olive oil and one part lemon make a healthy, pleasant-smelling polish.

Vacuum rugs once a week. Once a month, sprinkle them with baking soda—sweep it into the rug with a stiff broom and vacuum the baking soda. For heavy-duty cleaning, steam clean carpets with water, no solution needed. Treat animal protein stains, like vomit, feces, blood, or urine, by picking up solids, blotting excess liquid, covering with baking soda, and spraying white vinegar on it until it bubbles. Vacuum excess baking soda.

Gum erasers from the art supply store are made of natural rubber and are great for erasing "mistakes" on upholstery, wallpaper, matte-painted walls, and rugs.

To clean bodily fluids, other than blood, on mattresses or furniture, remove any solids, dip a rag into water and vinegar, spot clean, pour baking soda on the area, let it dry, and vacuum the baking soda; repeat as needed.

To clean blood on mattresses or furniture, spot clean by dabbing a wet cloth with a small amount of dish cleaner and continue dabbing with the clean areas of the cloth until the blood is gone. If the blood stains, pour a teaspoon of hydrogen peroxide directly on the spot, wait five minutes, and then dab with a dry cloth.

LAUNDRY

Toxins in laundry detergent consist of petrochemicals, including phosphates, naphthalene, or phenol. The wastewater from the detergent causes lakes, streams, and the ocean to have buildups of toxins, causing harm to aquatic life. Choosing natural, nonpoisonous products will keep your laundry clean without harming people, animals, and the planet.

Purchase biodegradable, nonpetroleum, phosphate-, fragrance-, dye-, and chlorine-free laundry detergent. Do not use more than is absolutely necessary. Buy powder instead of liquid detergent. Liquid detergent is made mostly of water, which costs more money to transport and package.

Separate loads, and only wash whites and extremely dirty loads with hot water.

Don't use bleach; it weakens fibers and has a negative effect when it reacts with other chemicals, forming toxic compounds that harm aquatic life.

Oxygen-based bleaches or a few cups of vinegar help boost a detergent's cleaning power.

For drying, use a clothesline when allowed and a drying rack when indoors. When air-drying laundry in a damp climate, fill shallow pans of garden lime to help absorb moisture. They can then be used in the garden when they are replaced every few weeks. Line drying in direct sun has the effect of a whitener without any chemicals. Don't line dry colors in direct sun; they will fade.

If you have to use a dryer, make sure it's an energy-efficient model. Something as simple as cleaning the lint before each load will greatly improve efficiency.

Don't use traditional dryer sheets. They contain a laundry list of carcinogenic toxins that can cause damage to vital organs and the respiratory, reproductive, and central nervous systems. A far healthier solution is to use vinegar. One half-cup in the rinse cycle will soften clothes and help eliminate static cling buildup in the dryer.

Try to avoid purchasing fabrics that need to be dry-cleaned. If you must dry-clean fabrics, use an eco-friendly dry-cleaner.

TRASH AND RECYCLING

In the '70s, people used to bring their bottles and cans back to the store for change. Now they just throw them away, even though in most states you pay an extra five or ten cents on each drink bottle you buy. We love to see resourceful people collecting these valuable materials from trash bins to bring them to a recycling plant. Eventually, when we run out of space to bury our trash, everything will be made of something that was recycled, and it will be mandatory that every product be recycled or able to decompose.

Unfortunately, we are not there yet. The recycling logistics are still a puzzle we are trying to solve. Plastic is our biggest problem—it's in most nonedible, disposable consumer products, it never biodegrades, and far too much of it is not recyclable. Even though most of it has a recycle symbol on it, not every region recycles every plastic. We are thrilled when we see

compostable plastics for dining and food wrappers. Thankfully, these materials are being used more and more often. Try to buy products that contain plastic that can be recycled in your area.

What Do the Different Numbers Inside of the Recycling Symbol Mean?

1. PETE (Polyethylene Terephthalate)
Uses: mouthwash, drinks, dish detergent, ketchup bottles
Recycles into: luggage, fabric, footwear, carpeting, fiberfill for clothes, bedding, sleeping bags

2. HDPE (High-Density Polyethylene)
Uses: drink jugs, detergent bottles
Recycles into: carpet, clothing, plant pots, detergent bottles, coat hangers, video cases, drainpipes, floor tiles, fencing, plastic lumber, road barriers

3. PVC (Polyvinyl Chloride)
Uses: plumbing pipes, vinyl siding, flooring and windows, electrical wire insulation
Recycles into: packaging, decking, paneling, mud flaps, flooring, speed bumps, floor mats

4. LDPE (Low-Density Polyethylene)
Uses: flexible lids, bottles
Recycles into: envelopes, garbage can liners, floor tiles, furniture, compost bins, trash cans, plastic lumber

5. PP (Polypropylene)
Uses: packaging, fabrics, car parts
Recycles into: auto battery cases, battery cables, brooms, ice scrapers, oil funnels, rakes, pallets

6. PS (Polystyrene)
Uses: Styrofoam, containers, lids, cups, bottles
Recycles into: light switch plates, thermal insulation, egg cartons, foam packaging, carryout containers, spray foam insulation

7. Other. Anything other than the previous six listed or a plastic made of two or more of the previous. Recycles into: plastic lumber, custom products

A home recycling center really amounts to nothing more than a few receptacles for different items. The most common trio includes a can for waste (trash), recyclables (metals, papers, plastics), and compost (food). Check with your municipality on how your area segregates recyclable items.

The EPA recommends waste prevention, recycling, and disposal for solid waste. A large amount of household waste comes from food that is thrown into the trash. Instead of tossing it out, recycle it. You've probably heard the term "composting." It's just the act of recycling food into nutrient-rich soil enhancer. Compost is also made of yard clippings. Recycle them too. Use biodegradable bags for the kitchen and yard waste.

If you have access to a yard, the compost can be used in the soil. In dense urban areas where yards are not common and one has no need for composted food waste, look for community gardens, botanical gardens, and farmers' markets that accept donated food scraps. Compost material must be plant based—no meat or bones please.

A little-known fact we picked up from Ellen Sandbeck's *Green Housekeeping* book is that you need to recycle paper in a timely manner. If you do not, it will become browned, brittle, and no longer suitable for recycling.

Things you place into a recycling bin must be clean, and lids, caps, and metal or plastic rings must be removed.

Don't store excess building materials. Get rid of them (donate, sell, or gift) because they evaporate, warp, and erode when they are not used for long periods. They then turn into trash.

If you receive a box filled with plastic peanuts, you can recycle them at the UPS Store and other box/shipping stores.

HAZARDOUS WASTE

The name pretty much says it all: hazardous waste. Most municipalities have facilities to deal with toxic waste. Check the internet for hazardous waste facilities in your area. Enter the name of your city or county followed by "hazardous waste drop-off" to view a list of facilities. When you are transporting items to the facility, do not mix them together in one container. Mixing chemicals can result in an explosion or fire. Keep them in their original containers if you can.

List of Hazardous Products
- Prescription drugs
- Paints (however, once they dry completely, you can throw them in the trash), solvents, thinners, strippers
- Pool and spa chemicals
- Fluorescent light bulbs
- Batteries
- Motor oil, antifreeze
- Poisons and pesticides

Never pour hazardous materials down drains, into gutters/storm sewers, into the trash, or on the ground. Properly disposing of hazardous waste helps to protect our waterways, groundwater, and soil. Burning your own trash is even worse. When plastic (which is in almost all trash) is burned, it releases dioxins. Waste facilities have high enough temperatures to eradicate dioxins, but individuals do not. It is also not safe to burn petroleum products, treated wood, or rubber.

Store all toxic chemicals far away from living spaces. Toxic chemicals such as paints, solvents, and cleaners are often stored in garages and basements. Make sure they are kept away from anything that can ignite flames. Encourage homeowners not to keep old chemicals in their homes but to dispose of them at hazardous waste facilities.

If there are going to be toxic products in the home, make sure to keep the labels on them in case of accidental poisoning. The list of ingredients may need to be conveyed to poison control.

Don't idle the car in a garage that is attached to a house. When the car has started, leave the structure, and turn it off as soon as the vehicle enters the garage.

Use rechargeable batteries. When they die or if you have dead disposables, dispose of or recycle them properly.

Although attractive from an energy conservation standpoint, fluorescent bulbs have mercury and are extremely toxic when improperly disposed of. Always bring them to an appropriate facility. (One more thing to love about IKEA—they have a cool recycling bin at all of their stores for batteries and fluorescent bulbs.)

Have furnaces cleaned by a professional at the beginning of the heating season.

Don't use the fireplace with the damper closed—carbon monoxide will fill the room. I was having a romantic glass of wine with a boyfriend one evening, and we didn't realize the damper was closed. We passed out from the carbon monoxide and thankfully were awakened by the fire department before we died. Don't learn the hard (embarrassing) way.

Electronics can be extremely hazardous when put into landfills. Check out the International Association of Electronics Recyclers (www.uia.org). Ask about the recycling program of the manufacturer when you purchase an electronic item.

Apparently, used inkjet cartridges and old cell phones are pretty valuable. There are many websites you can visit to collect cash for recycling these items. A few even have fundraising projects for nonprofit organizations. Wouldn't you rather give schoolkids your old cartridges and cell phones than buy another roll of overpriced wrapping paper?

Five Sources for Recycling and Purchasing Ink Cartridges and Electronics

- **Empties4Cash.** They buy your empty printer ink cartridges and even pay the shipping cost, making recycling effortless on your part.
- **Funding Factory.** Funding Factory is a nationwide fundraising organization, helping local communities recycle and generate income from doing so. They're also great because unlike many other programs, they also recycle toner.
- **Ink Jet Cartridges.** An excellent online retailer selling mostly printer refill kits across the US and Canada.
- **Gazelle.** Pays you $20 to $250 for used electronics like cell phones, computers, gaming consoles, and cameras, as long as the item isn't too old. Enter the model number on the site's calculator to find out what it's worth.
- **Earth911.** Locates a hazardous materials/recycling center near you.

OUTDOOR

What exactly is the problem with using synthetic pesticides, fertilizers, and herbicides, anyway? For decades, harmful chemical pesticides, fertilizers, and herbicides have been used all over the world, making most of the farmland soil unhealthy. When soil is treated with synthetic pesticides, fertilizers, and herbicides, the organic matter (earthworms and microorganisms) is killed.

These toxic chemicals also make the soil dry, which requires more of our precious freshwater supply to irrigate these crops. Soil with thriving organic matter pulls down carbon dioxide, which is digested by the microorganisms. This greatly reduces climate change. It also allows the organic matter to fertilize the soil, making it moist, healthy, and mineral rich for the next crop.

In order to eliminate the need for artificial pesticides and fertilizers, plant native species of flowers, grasses, trees, and shrubs. They will thrive in their natural climates, requiring less water, pesticides, fertilizers, and herbicides. This is because native species have adapted to pests in their climates.

Because composting encourages microorganisms to thrive, resulting in healthier soil, use it as a soil enhancer in place of fertilizer. Include a mix of brown materials (wood chips and straw) and green materials (kitchen scraps, lawn cuttings, leaves). If you need fertilizer, only use an organic variety once before the start of the growing season.

Don't use synthetic pesticides. Remove dead or diseased leaves immediately, and spray with an organic pesticide (or a crushed, strained garlic water spray) to keep disease from spreading. Remember that not all bugs are bad. Nematodes, ladybugs, and spiders are very happy to eat unwanted visitors. Spiders might be scary, but they sure do eat their fair share of pests. Beer, vinegar, and ducks are your first line of organic defense against snails. Beer attracts the slugs, then they drown, and the ducks find them very tasty. That good old vinegar spray also kills the slugs on contact. Throw the dead ones in the compost pile.

Kill weeds with vinegar spray, boiling water, or crushed rock salt. Use mulch very close to the bottom of plants to deter weeds from sprouting.

Mulch can also be placed on top of soil to help retain moisture (less need for watering) and reduce weeds (less need for herbicides). Mulch can be made of bark, wood chips, leaves, grass clippings, and pine needles and will need to be replaced every year because it breaks down into the soil. Around vegetable gardens, you can mulch with worn-out, used carpet that was made of natural materials (that's one way to keep it out of the landfill).

When fighting insects, a small pond filled with insect-eating fish is a much better solution to mosquito problems than chemical-laden citronella candles.

Create a rain garden. This is a small area of the yard that is at a lower level than the rest of it (four to five inches will work). When it rains or snows the rain garden will collect the water, allowing it to percolate into the soil instead of causing soil erosion or stormwater runoff into the waterways.

Clean gardening tools with vinegar and steel wool, and store them in a dry place or in sand. Keep tools sharp for better, easier cuts.

Don't waste water. Hoses should have trigger nozzles so they don't waste water while washing down patios or watering potted plants. Place water barrels under downspouts, and use the water for patio plants.

Use only biodegradable, chlorine- and phosphate-free products when cleaning your outdoor areas. This will prevent toxic water from running into waterways and into the soil.

To clean decks and outdoor furniture, spray with water, sprinkle baking soda all over the surface, work with a long-handled scrub brush or a handheld scrub brush, wait fifteen minutes, and rinse.

Make sure pools have a cover that keeps them clean and requires the use of fewer chemicals. Or, better, switch to saltwater pools.

Resources

- **www.naturalawn.com**—organic-based lawn care
- **www.cleanairgardening.com**—manual and electric lawn mowers, composting bins, and rain barrels
- **www.extremelygreen.com**—organic products
- **www.naturalinsectcontrol.com**—beneficial insects, traps, and barriers
- **www.groworganic.com**—tools and supplies for organic gardeners, organic growing supplies, natural fertilizers, organic pest control, and organic seeds
- **www.planetnatural.com**—garden and home supplies
- **www.seedsofchange.com**—organic seeds
- **www.gardensalive.com**—organic herbicides, pesticides, fertilizers, and environmentally responsible products

GLOSSARY

alternative energy—energy derived from natural sources that can be renewed at the same rate it is used. Some examples include sunlight, rain, tides, and geothermal heat.

American Society of Heating, Refrigeration, and Air-Conditioning Engineers (ASHRAE)—advances technology to serve humanity and promote a sustainable world.

bau-biologie—the study of how buildings affect human health. This knowledge is applied in green new construction, renovations, and remediation (fixing sick buildings).

biodegradable—the ability of soluble chemicals to break down into nontoxic ingredients that can go back into the earth or water systems.

carbon footprint—the total set of greenhouse gas emissions caused directly and indirectly by an individual, organization, event, or product.

carbon neutral—achieving net-zero carbon emissions by balancing a measured amount of carbon released with an equivalent amount of offset.

carcinogen—any substance or radiation that is an agent directly involved in the promotion of cancer.

certified organic—how the USDA defines organic production as a system that integrates cultural, biological, and mechanical practices that foster cycling of resources, promote ecological balance, and conserve biodiversity.

chlorine—a poisonous toxin that takes many years to evaporate while in the earth or water.

chlorofluorocarbons (CFCs)—widely used in aerosols, propellants, and refrigerants. They are believed to cause depletion of the ozone layer.

clean energy—a renewable energy source that does not pollute (wind, solar, geothermal, and hydrogen).

climate change—an increase in the earth's atmospheric and oceanic temperatures widely predicted to occur due to an increase in the greenhouse effect resulting especially from pollution.

composite boards—bonded waste wood from industrial processes or postconsumer recycled material that preferably contain no toxic materials.

compost—the decayed remains of organic matter that has rotted into a natural fertilizer.

Cradle to Cradle—a rating system developed by William McDonough and Dr. Michael Braungart that assesses products on a number of criteria, such as the use of safe and healthy materials, design for material reuse and recycling, efficient use of energy and water throughout production, and institution of strategies for social responsibility.

DEA free—does not contain DEA (diethanolamine), a substance linked to cancer.

dioxin—a highly carcinogenic chemical by-product formed during manufacturing and incineration of other chemicals which bioaccumulate in humans and animals due to its fat solubility.

ecolabel—a third-party certification that attests to the characteristics of a product and its low impact on the environment.

EcoLogo—a third-party certification of environmentally preferable products that was established in 1988.

emissions cap—a limit placed on companies regarding the amount of greenhouse gases they can emit.

energy efficient—a product that uses less energy than the same conventional product.

Energy Star—an EPA rating system for products that use energy. Energy Star–rated appliances meet the EPA's minimum energy-efficient standards.

Environmental Protection Agency (EPA)—an independent federal agency that was established to coordinate programs aimed at reducing pollution and protecting the environment.

fair trade—an organized social movement that helps producers in developing countries promote sustainability. Living wages, environmental and social standards, and a move toward economic independence and stability are the movement's main goals.

Forest Stewardship Council (FSC)—a nonprofit organization that sets certain high standards to ensure that forestry is practiced in an environmentally responsible and socially beneficial manner.

formaldehyde—a chemical carcinogen, known as a throat irritant and headache inducer.

FSC certified—a product label that means the wood used in the piece and the manufacturer that made it met the requirements of the FSC.

fuel cell—a technology that uses an electrochemical process to convert energy into electrical power.

Global Organic Textile Standards (GOTS)—a requirement that is used to ensure the organic status of textiles, from the harvesting of raw materials through environmentally and socially responsible manufacturing, packaging, labeling, exploration, and distribution in order to provide credible assurance to the end consumer.

green—philosophy supporting social, economic, and environmental sustainability.

green design—a philosophy of designing the built environment with the principles of economic, social, and environmental sustainability.

green energy—see *clean energy*.

Green Seal—an independent and nonprofit organization that evaluates and recommends products based on criteria that emphasize pollution prevention and environmentally responsible life cycle management. Eligible products are awarded the Green Seal.

Green-e Power—an independent, renewable energy certification and verification program allowing consumers to quickly identify environmentally superior energy options.

Greenguard—a certification program run by the Greenguard Environmental Institute (GEI), which establishes acceptable indoor air quality standards for products.

greenwashing—a superficial nod to the environment from marketers and businesses that historically were not interested in sustainable concerns in order to improve their public relation standing with the consumer or the public.

gray-water systems—systems that treat household wash water (all wastewater except toilet and garbage disposal) and reuse the water to irrigate landscaping and to flush toilets.

heat island effect—when heat islands form as vegetation is replaced by asphalt and concrete for roads, buildings, and other structures necessary to accommodate growing populations. These surfaces absorb rather than reflect the sun's heat, causing surface temperatures and overall ambient temperatures to rise.

Home Energy Rating System (HERS)—a system that involves an analysis of a home's construction plans and on-site inspections. This analysis yields a projected, preconstruction HERS Index. This index is subject to inspections of actual conditions once the project is completed.

Intergovernmental Panel on Climate Change (IPCC)—the leading body for the assessment of climate change, established by the United Nations.

International Organization for Standardization (ISO)—a third-party agency that specifies requirements for environmental management systems and social responsibility pertaining to fabric manufacturing.

landfill—an area designated to receive solid wastes, construction debris, household trash, and sludge from sewage treatment. A layer of soil is spread over the fill each day to reduce smell and health hazards. Well-run landfills are lined with plastic or clay to prevent toxins from entering the groundwater. Environmentalists dislike landfills because of their potential to pollute and the permanent removal of valuable raw materials.

Leadership in Energy and Environmental Design (LEED)—a green building rating system with an independent certification program that provides voluntary guidelines for developing high-performance, sustainable buildings. Created by the U.S. Green Building Council (USGBC), the program awards different levels of certification to buildings that meet LEED rating standards in five major categories: sustainable development, water savings, energy efficiency, material selections, and indoor environmental quality.

life cycle—the total impact of a system, function, product, or service from the extraction of raw materials through the end of its useful life.

light-emitting diodes (LED lights)—emit visible light when electricity is applied, much like a light bulb. LED lights use a fraction of the energy that fluorescent bulbs use to illuminate a space, and they can last for decades without replacements.

living wage—generally means that a person who works a forty-hour week, with no additional income, should be able to afford food, housing, utilities, health care, transportation, and recreation. This term does not mean minimum wage, which is a number set by law that may fail to meet the requirements of a living wage.

low-e windows—made of high-performance glass designed to reduce glare and heat gain for energy-efficient windows that offer clear views and energy savings.

no or low VOCs (volatile organic compounds)—VOCs are found in paints, sealers, paint strippers, and other solvents, including household cleaners. VOCs contribute to ground-level ozone and smog. Products that are below legal limits for their product class are called "low VOC" and products that test negative are called "no VOC."

nonrenewable resources—natural resources, like gas, coal, and oil, that once consumed cannot be replaced.

nontoxic—ingredients that pose no health risk.

Oeko-Tex Standard 100—introduced to the textile industry in Europe, this third-party agency specifies allowable levels in fabrics of potentially harmful substances that threaten human health.

off-gas—the term for the release of toxic gases from man-made materials.

organic—a term meaning no synthetic or chemical pesticides were used in growing a crop.

ozone layer—a naturally occurring atmospheric layer, roughly nine to thirty miles above the surface of the Earth, that forms a protective layer shielding the Earth from excess ultraviolet rays.

pesticides—chemicals used to kill insects and microorganisms.

petrochemical—a product made from petroleum.

phosphates—chemicals found in dishwashing and laundry detergent. When they are released into waterways via storm drains, they can produce excess growth of aquatic plants, which depletes oxygen levels and harms or kills aquatic life.

photovoltaic panels—solar panels that convert sunlight into electricity.

phthalates—industrial chemicals (plasticizers) that are frequently added to products to make plastic more flexible. They are suspected to be carcinogenic and hormone disruptors.

postconsumer waste—material that has been discarded after someone uses it.

preconsumer waste—material that has been discarded before it was ready for consumer use.

polyvinyl chloride (PVC)—the third most widely used thermoplastic polymer. Plasticizers that must be added to make PVC flexible have been of particular concern because some of these chemicals leach out of the vinyl products and are extremely toxic. DEHP is one of the most common toxic phthalate additives, as it is a suspected carcinogen and reproductive toxicant.

radiant heating—a system that supplies heat directly to the floor. The system relies on heat transfer, the delivery of heat from the hot surface to the people or animals in the room.

reclaimed materials—anything that was built and then reused for a new purpose.

recyclable—a product that after its intended use can be remade or manufactured into another useful material or product.

recycling—the act of processing used materials into new raw materials.

refurbished—the cleaning and reconditioning of useable parts.

renewable energy—see *clean energy*.

Restriction of Hazardous Substances (RoHS)—the directive on the restriction of the use of certain hazardous substances in electrical and electronic equipment. This directive restricts the use of six hazardous materials in the manufacture of various types of electronic and electrical equipment. It is closely linked with the waste electrical and electronic equipment directive, which sets collection, recycling, and recovery targets for electrical goods and is part of a legislative initiative to solve the problem of huge amounts of toxic e-waste.

Scientific Certification Systems (SCS)—a leading third-party provider of certification, auditing, and testing services and standards, founded in 1984.

sick building syndrome—a combination of ailments caused by exposure to toxins in a residence usually resulting from poor indoor air quality.

Skal—a well-respected Dutch nonprofit that certifies worldwide organic agriculture and production.

structured insulated panels (SIPS)—a composite material consisting of two layers of structural board with insulation in between that shares the same properties as an I-beam.

sustainable—using a resource so it is not depleted or permanently damaged.

Sustainable Furniture Council—a nonprofit organization of suppliers, manufacturers, retailers, and designers formed to promote sustainable practices in the furniture industry.

triple bottom line—sustainable business practice that involves the pursuit of three goals: economic profit, ecological integrity, and social equity instead of a single, financial bottom line.

United States Green Building Council (USGBC)—a nonprofit community of leaders working to make green buildings available to everyone. Council members work together to develop industry standards, design, and construction practices as well as guidelines, operating practices, policy positions, and educational tools that support the adoption of sustainable design and building practices. Members also forge strategic alliances with industry and research organizations, federal government agencies, and state and local governments to transform the built environment. As the leading organization that represents the entire building industry on environmental building matters, USGBC's unique perspective and collective power enable members to effect change in the way buildings are designed, built, operated, and maintained. The USGBC's greatest strength is the diversity of its membership. USGBC is a balanced, consensus nonprofit organization representing the entire building industry, comprising more than twelve thousand companies and organizations. Since its inception in 1993, USGBC has played a vital role in providing a leadership forum and a unique, integrating force for the building industry.

volatile organic compounds (VOCs)—found in paints, sealers, paint strippers, and other solvents, including household cleaners, VOCs contribute to ground-level ozone and smog.

WaterSense—a partnership sponsored by the US Environmental Protection Agency that makes it easy for Americans to save water and protect the environment by labeling these products with a WaterSense logo.

INDEX

Books from Allworth Press

Art Collecting Today
by Doug Woodham (6 × 9, 208 pages, paperback, $19.99)

Business and Legal Forms for Interior Designers, Second Edition
by Tad Crawford and Eva Doman Bruck (8½ × 11, 288 pages, paperback, $29.95)

The Challenge of Interior Design
by Mary V. Knackstedt (6 × 9, 272 pages, paperback, $24.95)

Design Thinking
by Thomas Lockwood (6 × 9, 304 pages, paperback, $24.95)

Designers Don't Read
by Austin Howe (5½ × 8½, 224 pages, paperback, $19.95)

Feng Shui and Money, Second Edition
by Eric Shaffert (6 × 9, 256 pages, paperback, $19.99)

Green Graphic Design
by Brian Dougherty with Celery Design Collaborative (6 × 9, 212 pages, paperback, $24.95)

How to Think Like a Great Graphic Designer
by Debbie Millman (6 × 9, 248 pages, paperback, $24.95)

Interior Design Clients
by Thomas L. Williams (6 × 9, 256 pages, paperback, $24.95)

Interior Design Practice
by Cindy Coleman (6 × 9, 256 pages, paperback, $24.95)

Interior Designer's Guide to Pricing, Estimating, and Budgeting, Second Edition
by Theo Stephan Williams (6 × 9, 256 pages, paperback, $24.95)

The Joy of Art
by Carolyn Schlam (8 × 10, 352 pages, hardcover, $34.99)

The Law (in Plain English)® for Collectors
by Leonard D. DuBoff and Sarah J. Tugman (6 × 9, 240 pages, paperback, $19.99)

The Law (in Plain English)® for Small Business, Fifth Edition
by Leonard D. DuBoff and Amanda Bryan (6 × 9, 312 pages, paperback, $24.99)

Marketing Interior Design, Second Edition
by Lloyd Princeton (6 × 9, 224 pages, paperback, $24.95)

Quadrant Life
by Lori Dennis with Foreword by Farah Merhi (5½ × 8¼, 216 pages, hardcover, $16.99)

Starting Your Career as a Contractor
by Claudiu Fatu (6 × 9, 224 pages, paperback, $19.99)

Starting Your Career as an Interior Designer, Second Edition
by Robert K. Hale and Thomas L. Williams (6 × 9, 252 pages, paperback, $19.99)

Your Architecture Career
by Gary Unger (6 × 9, 208 pages, paperback, $19.99)

To see our complete catalog or to order online, please visit www.allworth.com.